CAST IN GOD'S IMAGE

OTHER BOOKS BY HOWARD A. ADDISON

The Enneagram and Kabbalah: Reading Your Soul
(JEWISH LIGHTS)

*Show Me Your Way: The Complete Guide to Exploring
Interfaith Spiritual Direction*
(SKYLIGHT PATHS)

CAST IN GOD'S IMAGE

Discover Your Personality Type
Using the Enneagram and Kabbalah

HOWARD A. ADDISON

For People of All Faiths, All Backgrounds

JEWISH LIGHTS Publishing

Woodstock, Vermont

Cast in God's Image:
Discover Your Personality Type Using the Enneagram and Kabbalah

© 2001 by Howard A. Addison

Library of Congress Cataloging-in-Publication Data

Addison, Howard A., 1950–
Cast in God's image : discover your personality type using the enneagram and kabbalah / Howard A. Addison.
p. cm.
Includes bibliographical references.
ISBN 1-58023-124-1 (Papberback)
1. Typology (Psychology)—Religious aspects—Judaism. 2. Enneagram.
3. Cabala—History. 4. Spiritual life. I. Title.
BM538.P68 A37 2001
296.7—dc21   2001004586

10 9 8 7 6 5 4 3 2 1

Manufactured in the United States of America

For People of All Faiths, All Backgrounds
Published by Jewish Lights Publishing
A Division of LongHill Partners, Inc.
Sunset Farm Offices, Route 4, P.O. Box 237
Woodstock, VT 05091
Tel: (802) 457-4000   Fax: (802) 457-4004

www.jewishlights.com

To Bahira Chava
the one who brings radiance and life.

CONTENTS

PROLOGUE

I t hardly seems that three years have passed since the release of my previous work, *The Enneagram and Kabbalah: Reading Your Soul.* In the intervening years, I have been gratified by the response to that comparative study. Recognizing the root of one's soul—and that of others—is a powerful first step toward personal growth and improved relationships. In both religious and secular settings, individuals ranging in age from young teenagers through older seniors have appreciated how these two systems of sacred psychology enhance each other, and help map our journey of human development and spiritual discovery.

The impetus to write this book, *Cast in God's Image*, came from two sources. The first was as a response to readers of *The Enneagram and Kabbalah* who said, "Rabbi, I finished your book, but I still can't figure out my type." The initial sections of *Cast in God's Image* are specifically geared to serve as an entry for those encountering the Enneagram for the first time. My second motivation derives from the core imagery of the Lurianic Kabbalah. This mystical teaching indicates that there are sparks of holiness scattered throughout the world, which each of us alone as unique individuals can elevate. The spiritual exercises in the latter sections of the book are designed to help readers identify which of the sparks are especially theirs as they prepare for the next chapter of their lives. These exercises have formed the basis of workshops I have conducted over these last years and have proved to be both moving and helpful to those who have tried them. (Note: If you are already sure of your type, you might wish to go directly to Part Three.)

The Talmud indicates that those who credit their sources help bring salvation to the world. In that spirit, let me first thank my teachers, Helen Palmer and David Daniels. Their groundbreaking work describing the shift from higher to lower consciousness, the shift from the realm of Essence to Personality, and the path by which we can convert our vices into virtues inform much of this text. The "Could This Be You?" tales in chapters 4 through 12 have been adapted from attentional exercises that we, the students, developed at their workshops.

Additional thanks are due to Don Richard Riso, who discovered the Levels of Development in 1977. He and his co-author, Russ Hudson, have worked out nine distinct levels for each type, grouped by healthy, average, and unhealthy ranges. They have also done extensive investigation into the effect the *wings* have on each core personality type. For more information, see Riso and Hudson, *Personality Types* (Revised edition. Boston: Houghton Mifflin, 1996).

Renee Baron, Elizabeth Wagele, and Helen Peacock have helped make discovering one's personality type fun through the use of cartooning and songs. Along with all Enneagram students, I am in their debt for injecting elements of humor into what threatens to be an overly serious realm of study.

I thank Jewish Lights Publishing and their editorial duo, the two Emilys—Emily Bloch and Emily Wichland—for their literary suggestions and for shepherding this project through. Finally, to Donna Rosenthal—whose research assistance, manuscript preparation, and keen insights have helped make this book a reality—my deepest thanks.

May the teachings and exercises that follow help you uncover that spark of divine truth that is uniquely yours. In turn, may you then manifest that truth for your own growth and for the healing and growth of our world.

Rabbi Howard Avruhm Addison

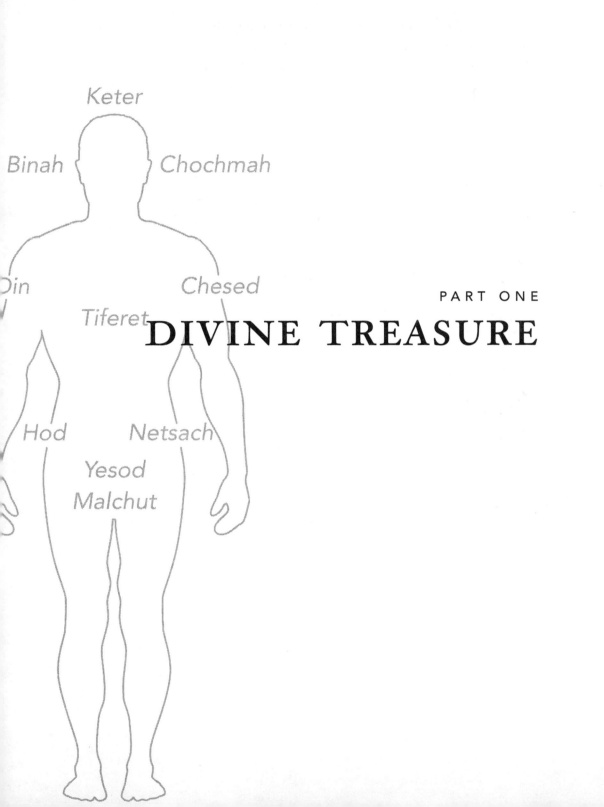

PART ONE

DIVINE TREASURE

1

Children of the King

Many years ago, and in a faraway place, a powerful king lived in a splendid palace. Although the king ruled many lands and possessed great wisdom and wealth, his son was his chief delight. Each and every day he would talk to, teach, and play with the boy. He marveled at his son's growth and development.

As the prince grew into a young man, the king realized that it was time for his son to go out on his own. After all, how else could the boy develop independent judgment and a sense of himself? Just before the prince left, his father said, "My child, know wherever you go, whatever you do, that you are my son and always will be. No matter where you travel, never forget—you are the child of a king."

The son journeyed far and wide. While he met with some success, for the first time he also experienced hurt and failure. His companions took advantage of him and squandered his wealth. As his life unraveled he forgot his former life and his father, the king.

Word came to the king about his son's pitiful state. Determined to see for himself, the king set off, stopping at each tavern and gambling house, seeking news of his child. After crossing a dark forest he finally saw a hut standing by a stream. Knocking on the door he entered and saw his shivering son. The tearful father shook his head and asked, "My child, don't you know me? What can I do for you?"

The young man looked up, no hint of recognition in his dull eyes, "Sir, I'm very cold. Could you possibly spare a warm blanket and a pair of shoes? These, more than anything, are what I need."[1]

Each time I read this tale I wonder how much we, the women and men of today, are like that shivering son. Rabbi Israel Baal Shem Tov (d.1760), the founder of Chasidism, stated that the greatest sin we can commit is to forget that we are children of the King, children of God. Yet, in our desire to just survive the hassles of daily living, we repeat this sin again and again. Life can be so cold, our path so bumpy, that a little added warmth and ease can seem like the greatest of gifts. Who has the time or energy to think about things like true identities, noble deeds, our kinship with God—and what all of these things might call us to do?

Living in an era of constant fluctuation can make it difficult just to keep pace. Social roles that once seemed firm and defined have been displaced by a host of lifestyles from which to choose. While these are liberating for many, the sheer variety of choices can make us feel insecure, as if we constantly have to make up our lives as we go along. Technical skills acquired yesterday become obsolete tomorrow. The decisions and blunders of far-off governments or corporations can threaten our livelihood and wreak havoc on our lives. Even the support of extended family, once a cushion against such shocks, can no longer be relied upon as we move away from loved ones in search of new opportunities.

Given that these personal and professional relationships can be so fleeting—sometimes against our will—it's little wonder that we hurt. But the way we manage this pain is now changing in a strange way. Rather than trying to heal and move forward with their lives, many people seem to retain their wounds, if not celebrate them. Personal problems that we would have hesitated to divulge to our closest friends a generation ago are today broadcast on call-in radio programs and television talk shows. Terms like "compulsive," "recovering from," or "survivor of" are part of everyday speech and are commonly used in describing ourselves and others.

Why? Perhaps because such shorthand labels give us a feeling of knowledge and authority without requiring us to look too closely at someone else or at ourselves. Perhaps we think our pain entitles us to extra sympathy or excuses unacceptable behavior. Or perhaps our past wounds might now be such crucial elements of our identity that giving them up would raise such scary questions as "Who am I?" and "What have I been called to do?"

The story of the king's son reminds us that there is more in our lives than blankets and shoes to protect us against life's chills and bumps. Like the king, God just may be inviting us to reestablish our kinship and reclaim our identities as daughters and sons of God. By learning from the varied images, lessons, and applied practices of two related sacred psychologies—Kabbalah, the Jewish mystical tradition, and the nine-pointed Enneagram of personality types—we might just be able to reveal the Divine within us and discover sacred tasks that are uniquely ours to perform in this world.

2
God's Currency

The first chapter of Genesis indicates that we humans, men and women, are created in "the image of God" (Genesis 1:27). Yet, all we have to do is look at our neighbors, our coworkers, and our loved ones to realize that no two people are exactly alike. An ancient rabbinic parable speaks directly to our uniqueness as human beings:

> A ruler of flesh and blood stamps coins from the same mold, and each turns out the same. The Holy One also stamps coins from the same mold, yet each differs from all the rest.[1]

It is clear that we are the divine coins referred to above, shaped through the mold of the first couple, Adam and Eve. Much as metal coins bear a seal or the image of a national leader, so are we imprinted with an image: the image of God. However, while currency of the same denomination appears identical, the parable suggests that each man and woman is distinct, never exactly seen before and never to be quite repeated again.

If we are all created in God's image, what might account for our differences? How can we identify those traits that make us distinct? If we are not only God's children but God's currency, how do we determine our own intrinsic value and that which we, and we alone, are meant to redeem? Perhaps the answers to these ultimate questions might unfold if we begin at the beginning.

CREATION

The first three Hebrew words of the Bible are *Beresheet Bara Elohim.* If translated in sequence, they literally mean, "In the beginning created God." If God is eternal, without beginning or end, in what possible way can we say that God was created? According to Kabbalah, the Jewish mystical tradition, a sublime creative process occurred within God at the same time God formed our physical world.

The name by which Kabbalists refer to God's essential nature is *Ayn Sof,* "Boundless" or "Without End." If *Ayn Sof* is infinite, all-enveloping, seamless, and mysterious, it is also unknowable. As limited physical beings we recognize other beings and objects by their boundaries, marking where one thing leaves off and another begins; we are unable to identify the essential nature of God. Therefore, if we, God's creatures, are to recognize and respond to our Creator, God needed to project the contours of a divine personality we humans might be able to perceive, if not fully grasp.

Jewish mysticism refers to ten different aspects of God's personality. The Tree of Life, *Etz Chayim,* is made up of these aspects, or *sefirot.* Each *sefirah* is described as follows:

Keter, Supernal Crown: The transition from potential to actuality, from the unknowable *Ayn Sof* to God's revealed personality. *Keter* has been compared to the point where a pen touches the paper before any writing begins.

Chochmah, Wisdom: The encapsulation of all perfect possibilities before those possibilities unfold. Since *Chochmah's* pristine content is encoded much the way DNA is encoded within a seed, this *sefirah* is also referred to as *Abba,* Supernal Father.

Binah, Understanding: The ability to discern different realities and needs and to respond accordingly. Since "being" differentiates within *Binah* into the ideal forms of objects and creatures the way a zygote develops into a fetus of organs and limbs within the womb, *Binah* is also called *Ima,* Supernal Mother.

Gedulah, Greatness: The creative force of God's love, also known as *Chesed,* the higher expressions of loyalty, kindness, and piety.

Din, Judgment: The aspect of God that sets limits and boundaries. *Din* is to *Chesed* as form is to content. Also called *Gevurah*, the manifestation of divine power.

Tiferet, Beauty: The beauty that emerges when *Chesed* and *Din* are in balance. In our unredeemed world, *Tiferet* embodies a yearning for completion and equilibrium.

Netsach, Endurance: The enduring, steadfast nature of God. *Netsach* filters the divine grace of *Gedulah* and helps channel that expansive, creative energy to the lower world.

Hod, Splendor: Divine majesty or splendor. *Hod* refracts and conveys the defining energy of *Din* to the lower world, thus keeping the forces of chaos and entropy at bay.

Yesod, Foundation: Also known as *Tsadik*, Righteous, because "the righteous are the foundation of the world" (Proverbs 10:25). *Yesod* focuses the divine energy, *Shefa*, from the higher *sefirot* and channels it downward.

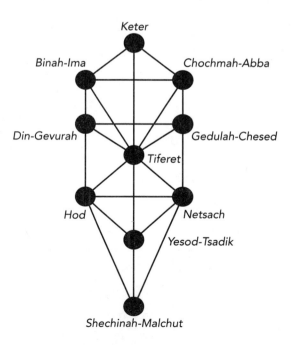

8

Yesod symbolizes the male generative organ when the *sefirot* are depicted in human form (see *Adam Kadmon*, page 10).

Shechinah, Accepting Presence: God's accepting presence, which receives the *Shefa*, divine energy, from *Tiferet* and *Yesod* and mediates its blessings to our world. Like *Binah*, it is a feminine aspect of God and is described as a sister or bride. The closest *sefirah* to our world, *Shechinah* symbolizes God's nearness and is also referred to as *Malchut*, divine sovereignty.

Kabbalists have offered a variety of models to explain the mysterious relationship between *Ayn Sof* and the *sefirot*. Perhaps it is best to think of the *sefirot* as being similar to a jewel's facets: the different external features of the same gem, the *Ayn Sof*.

IN GOD'S IMAGE

For Kabbalists, the term "the image of God" is more than a figure of speech. It is a symbol that graphically reflects God's nature and ours. As an alternative to the *Etz Chayim*, Jewish mystics actually depicted the *sefirot* in human form. Drawing on an ancient rabbinic legend, they called this figure Primordial Adam, *Adam Kadmon*.

Not only can God's personality be represented by our human structure, but conversely, each of our own souls contains the potential of all the *sefirot*. However, our different temperaments and personalities derive, in part, from the fact that each of our souls finds its ultimate source in one particular *sefirah*. Only the soul of the Messiah will emanate from the Supernal Crown, *Keter*, which is the highest *sefirah*. The rest of us each find our own *shoresh neshamah*, the root of our individual souls, in one of the nine remaining *sefirot*.

UNCOVERING THE ROOT OF YOUR SOUL

If every soul is derived from one of the nine lower *sefirot*, why do there seem to be as many variations of the human personality as there are humans? And why, if our spirits are rooted in divinity, isn't that divinity readily apparent to us and to others? The answer to both questions lies in the single Hebrew word *tselem*, or image.

Kabbalists envisioned the *tselem* as an ethereal body that intervenes between our souls and our physical being. If the *tselem* is thought of as a garment, then it is woven throughout our lives and is made up of our character traits, our values, and our experiences. And just like a custom-made garment, this acquired personality can both cloak and reveal the divine reality of our soul, which lies underneath.

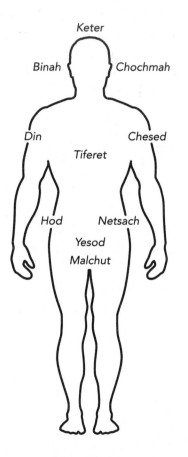

Adam Kadmon
(Primordial Adam)

Rabbinic psychology claims that we have not one conscience but two character inclinations: the *Yetser Ha Tov*, our good, altruistic inclination, and the *Yetser Ha Ra*, our harmful and self-aggrandizing inclination. According to tradition, God fashioned both of these in the human being with the same creative act.[2] Therefore, our virtues and vices are not really the opposites of each other, but their flip sides. For example, a helpful person might offer assistance to another not only because it is needed but to gain praise and perhaps to manipulate the person being helped. Thus, our *tselem* is composed of our radiant qualities and also the truncated, dark side of our traits known as the *tsel*, or shadow.

How can we recognize the light-and-shadow characteristics particular to our *tselem*, which might help us identify the particular *sefirah* that is our *shoresh neshamah*, the root of our soul, covered by our *tselem*? For this task we can call on a system of sacred psychology that shares many sources and insights with Kabbalah: the Enneagram.[3]

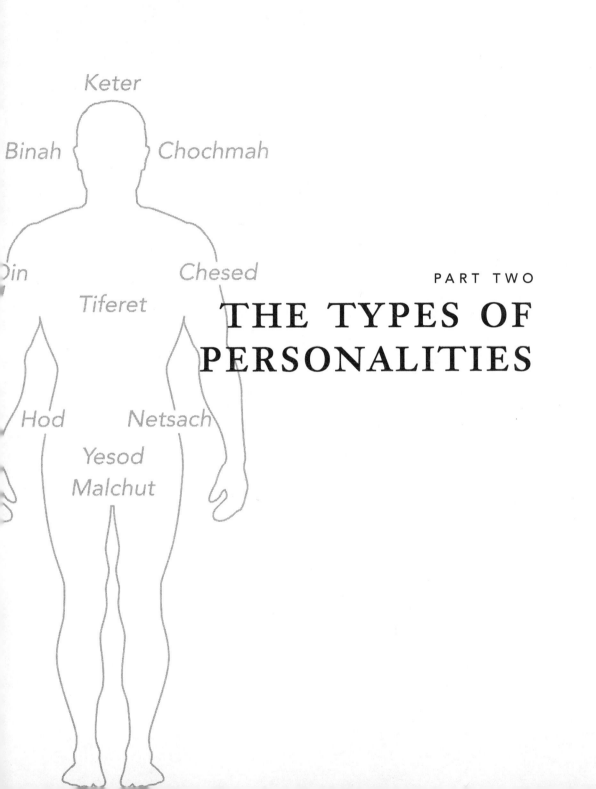

Keter

Binah · Chochmah

Din · Chesed

Tiferet

Hod · Netsach

Yesod
Malchut

PART TWO

THE TYPES OF PERSONALITIES

3
Nine Points

AT FIRST GLANCE

Enneagram is a Greek word meaning "nine points." Each of the nine points represents a different basic personality type, people who share a similar perspective on life and have the same underlying motivations. Differences among people of the same type might derive from gender, age, level of personal growth, societal values, or other factors.[1] The insights of the Enneagram can broaden our perspective by helping us recognize and understand our own patterns of behavior and those of the people around us. They can free us to explore responses different from the usual ways we react to situations and allow us to view the conduct and outlook of others with greater sympathy.

THE DIAGRAM

When the Enneagram is drawn, it is a starlike figure enclosed by a circle. This visual map allows us to plot the nine basic personality types and chart their dynamic interactions.

Contours

The nine points of the Enneagram are actually composed of two different shapes: an equilateral triangle and a six-pointed figure.

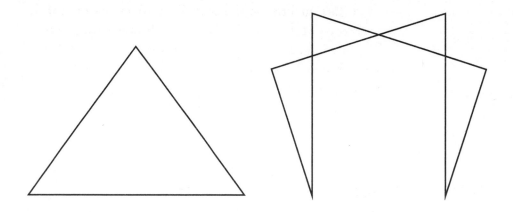

When the two shapes are superimposed one upon the other and a circle is drawn around them, the Enneagram looks like this:

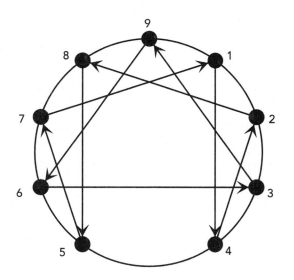

Lines

Each point on the Enneagram is connected by lines to two other points. Those connecting lines are your *arrows*. When you face undue pressure, you often take on the more negative traits of the number toward which your arrow lies, known as your *stress point*. When you are feeling at ease, you tend to display the more positive qualities of the type directed away from the arrow's tip, called your *security point*. In some instances, however, our response to stress can actually motivate us to take on some positive aspects of our stress point; conversely, the inability to deal well with ease can bring out some negative traits of our security point.

STRESS POINT	CORE TYPE		CORE TYPE	SECURITY POINT
Romantic 4 ←	1	Perfectionist	1 ←	7 Adventurer
Confronter 8 ←	2	Caregiver	2 ←	4 Romantic
Mediator 9 ←	3	Achiever	3 ←	6 Loyal Cynic
Caregiver 2 ←	4	Romantic	4 ←	1 Perfectionist
Adventurer 7 ←	5	Observer	5 ←	8 Confronter
Achiever 3 ←	6	Loyal Cynic	6 ←	9 Mediator
Perfectionist 1 ←	7	Adventurer	7 ←	5 Observer
Observer 5 ←	8	Confronter	8 ←	2 Caregiver
Loyal Cynic 6 ←	9	Mediator	9 ←	3 Achiever

The arrows indicate that the Enneagram is a dynamic system. Rather than placing us in neat, stagnant categories, it helps us understand how our basic personality traits change under more extreme conditions. (For instance, when people ask, "What got into Joe today?" that indicates that Joe's basic personality has changed under stress or while at ease.) They can also be helpful as we seek to identify our own type, and they are useful as tools for personal growth.

Wings

Surrounding the nine Enneagram points is a circle, which demonstrates that our core personality type is also influenced by the points on either side.

These neighboring types are referred to as our *wings*. Usually one of the two wings is predominant and exerts a distinct influence on our personality. Whereas the manifestations of our stress and security points are situational, the impact of the predominant wing is fairly constant. We might compare a point's wings to the two profiles of a face—both are there and can be accessed, but one is usually the stronger and is more preferred.

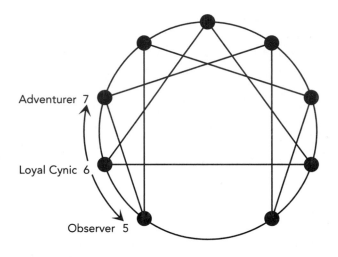

The wings of type 6 are 5 and 7

NINE POINTS: A TYPE-BY-TYPE SYNOPSIS

1. *Perfectionists* are objective, idealistic, and conscientious. Concerned with order and correctness, they can be overly critical as they strive to excel and live by their own high standards.

2. *Caregivers* are friendly, empathetic, and generous. They can adapt their personality to meet others' needs while often not recognizing their own.

3. *Achievers* are practical, competitive, and energetic. At times deceptive to themselves and to others, they are interested in maintaining a winning image, and they work hard for recognition and prestige.

4. *Romantics* are introspective and sensitive, and they appreciate the artistic and the beautiful. They live with passionate feelings and are given to changes of mood, melancholy, and romantic longing.

5. *Observers* are rational, insightful, and most comfortable when analyzing ideas and principles. Appearing detached and outwardly unemotional, they are independent people of modest needs who thirst for knowledge.

6. *Loyal Cynics* are dependable and equitable. Faithful to family, friends, and causes, they are suspicious about the motives of others, particularly those in charge. Viewing the world as a fearful place, some withdraw from perceived threats (phobic), while others rush into challenges head-long (counterphobic).

7. *Adventurers* are optimistic, joyous, and spontaneous. Possessing a wide variety of interests and abilities, they sometimes ignore pitfalls and limitations while looking to life's bright side.

8. *Confronters* are assertive, forceful, and unwilling to submit. Concerned with power and control, they can be strong leaders, particularly when fighting injustice.

9. *Mediators* are easygoing, patient, and accepting. At times passively aggressive and stubborn, they can see the validity of varying points of view and seek peace by harmonizing differences.

THE TRIADS

We all relate to the world by instinct, feeling, and reason. However, given our own personality inclinations, we each tend to emphasize one of these faculties over the other two.

The Enneagram's nine points are divided into three groups of three, called *triads*. Discovering which triad is yours can be helpful in recognizing the primary way you react to the world and in identifying your personality type.

Instinctual

The instinctual (gut) types are at points Eight, Nine, and One. People in this group often experience bodily sensations or "gut feelings" before they

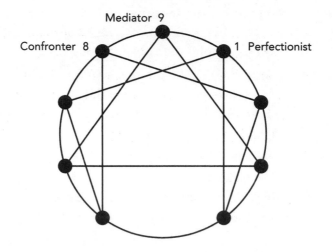

The Instinctual Triad: types 8, 9 and 1

actually can tell what they think or feel about a new situation. The energy of this triad is the energy to "stand against," as can be shown in the aggressiveness of the Confronter (8), the stubbornness of the Mediator (9), and the critical nature of the Perfectionist (1).

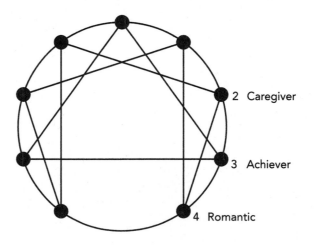

The Feeling Triad: types 2, 3 and 4

Feeling

The feeling (heart) types are at points Two, Three, and Four. The energy of people in this triad is the energy to "move toward," to gauge others' feelings and how others feel about them. They can respond emotionally to new situations before they recognize what they think or how they should react. Caregivers (2) want to be loved and to be perceived as being helpful; Achievers (3) want to be admired and to project a winning image; Romantics (4) want to be understood as being special.

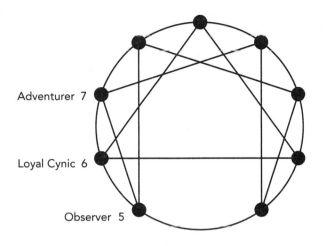

The Thinking Triad: types 5, 6 and 7

Thinking

The thinking (head) types are points Five, Six, and Seven. People in this triad think of the world as an intrusive, fearful, or limiting place. When faced with a new situation, they tend to analyze, evaluate, or plan before responding with action or feeling. Their energy is the energy to "move within." Observers (5) can isolate themselves in thought. Loyal Cynics (6) pull back before either escaping from or rushing into perceived danger. Adventurers (7) might withdraw from previously made commitments in search of more exciting exploits.

A friend told me the following story that perfectly illustrates the differences among the triads. She and two other women had gone to the beach. Upon returning to the spot where they thought they had parked, they discovered the car was gone.

"Our car's been stolen!" cried the first woman, at once becoming distraught.

"Let's assess the situation," coolly responded my friend, a thoughtful type.

"Assess the &$%#*% situation!!? Our car has been stolen!" the agitated woman yelled, incredulously.

Suddenly the third of the group strode off purposefully. "Where are you going?" the other two asked.

"To find the car and whoever took it," was the reply.

As it happened, the car had actually been parked in the next block, but the first response of each woman was true to triad form: the heart-based first woman became emotional, my head-centered friend started to think it through, the instinctual third woman naturally moved into action.

LOCATING YOUR POINT

Now that we've looked at some of the Enneagram's guidelines, the next chapters will assist you in determining your own type. After reading each of chapters 4 through 12, fill out each chapter's "Taking Stock" checklist. Answer each question by remembering what you were like in your late teens through mid-twenties (if you're past that age), when your behavioral responses were more natural and less self-reflective. Next, go back and reread those types that yielded the highest scores. See if one of those types best describes you. If you still can't decide between different types, try the following:

1. Identify the triad in which each is found, and see which coincides with your predominant way of reacting: Instinctual (8, 9, and 1), Feeling (2, 3, and 4), or Thinking (5, 6, and 7).

2. Look closely at the descriptions of the wings of each type you are considering. If you feel that you share several characteristics with the wings of one point under consideration but not with those of the other, the one between the wings with which you identify might well be your type.

For example, if you can't choose between type Six (Loyal Cynic) and One (Perfectionist) and you share traits with types Five (Observer) and Seven (Adventurer) but not with Nine (Mediator) and Two (Caregiver), then Six might be your type.

3. Look at the arrows and examine the stress points and security points of those types you are considering. Again, the type whose stress point best reflects how your personality changes under pressure and whose security point best depicts how you act when at ease might be your core type. If you become quite adventurous and carefree when feeling secure (7, Adventurer) and are given to feeling worthless and acting maudlin when under stress (4, Romantic) chances are you might be type One, a Perfectionist.

After all things are considered, it is only you who can identify your type. Most people report a simultaneous feeling of "Aha!" and "Oh, no!" when they confront the virtues and shortcomings of the type that is truly their own.

4

Point One: The Perfectionist

COULD THIS BE YOU?

You are seated in the waiting area of a restaurant. It is now 12:18 P.M., and for the umpteenth time, Joe is late. Your simmer slowly rises to a boil as you recall each time Joe kept you waiting, where it occurred, and for how long.

"How inconsiderate can he be? I left an important meeting to be here on time. My schedule is much busier than his, and I made it. Why does he think he can get away with not keeping promises? It's just not right! I keep my word even if it kills me!"

At 12:30 Joe strolls in, a full thirty minutes late. You'd love to explode but are proud to say you have too much self-control for such an open display of anger. Feeling bubbling resentment, you wait for him to apologize profusely while you offer an icy greeting as a punishment.

Finally you're seated at your table. You take a deep breath to let some tension go. Looking down at the place setting, you automatically notice that there is a spot on the teaspoon and your napkin is out of place. . . .

Perfectionists are:

AT BEST	AS TENSION BUILDS	AT WORST
Conscientious and moral	Critical	Self-righteous
Responsible	Moralizing	Intolerant
Hardworking	Resentful	Angry
Honest and just	Insistent on protocol	Dogmatic
Faithful to principle	Bent on improving others	Paralyzed by the quest for perfection

TAKING STOCK

Check the statements that best describe you in your late teens to mid-twenties.

☐ It's very important for me to get things right. If not, I feel as if my world might fall apart.

☐ I think of myself as an ethical, highly principled person.

☐ Keeping commitments is very important to me.

☐ While I can be critical of others, I am most critical of myself.

☐ My attention is naturally drawn toward flaws that need to be corrected.

☐ Leisure and recreation time should be earned.

☐ I feel anger and resentment when I think someone is "getting away" with something.

☐ Since the time I was young I've been the responsible one, the "good boy" or "good girl."

☐ I often see things as black or white, with little room for shades of gray.

☐ I express my concern for others by trying to help them be the best they can be.

☐ I try to avoid showing anger or resentment even when others are unjust or unreliable.

☐ I often feel stuck between something I know is right (but which I don't want) and doing what I want (which may not be right).

☐ Integrity and fairness are very important to me.

☐ I strive for order and punctuality.

☐ I often feel tense and worried, as if a "little critic" were sitting on my shoulder.

BLESSINGS OF BEING A PERFECTIONIST

- I am honest and will not betray my moral standards.
- I maintain high ideals and am dedicated to improving myself and the world around me.
- I am dependable and industrious.

DIFFICULTIES OF BEING A PERFECTIONIST

- My desire to always "get it right" can make me feel tense, anxious, and lonely.
- I can become so caught up in the details that it slows or paralyzes my work.
- My criticisms can hurt others, making them feel inferior or rejected, dampening their joy or my own.

WINGS

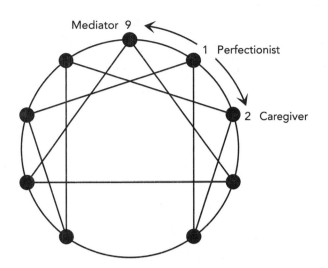

The wings of type 1 are 9 and 2

Your core personality type can be influenced by the points adjacent to yours. Usually one of the wings is stronger and can have a distinct effect on your personality.

Perfectionists with a pronounced Nine (Mediator) wing can seem more tranquil and even remote. While their judgment can be measured and equitable, at times their perspective seems impersonal and their standards unreachable.

Perfectionists with a pronounced Two (Caregiver) wing can seem more humane and giving of themselves to help others. At times more understanding and forgiving, they can also become scolding and authoritarian.

ARROWS

When feeling secure, Perfectionists can display tendencies of the Seven (Adventurer).

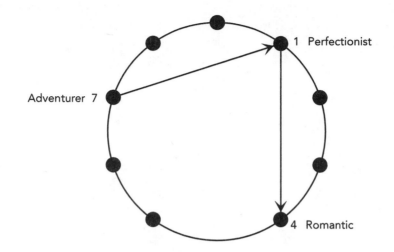

Positive Traits

- You become more spontaneous and playful.
- You can have fun rather than concentrating on what you "ought" to do.
- You can be more self-affirming and less self-critical.

Negative Trait

- You can drown out your critical mind with an excess of food, sex, or substance abuse.

When under stress, Perfectionists move towards Four (Romantic).

Negative Traits

- Rather than seeing your actions as flawed, you might view *yourself* as worthless and flawed.
- You can channel your anger inwardly, becoming maudlin and depressed.
- Your feelings may become so overpowering that you can't see reality clearly and you overdramatize your plight.

Positive Trait

- Rather than dealing with your own "oughts" and others' notions of who you should be, you can get in touch with your own deepest feelings.

AS A CHILD

- You were the "good girl" or "good boy" who tried to live up to your parents' and teachers' expectations.
- You were the "responsible one," taking on obligations at home at a young age.
- Doing the "right thing" was expected. You were criticized or punished for mistakes—but not always rewarded for doing good.
- You learned that it was inappropriate to show anger.
- You won approval for being correct, having high standards, working hard, and seeking excellence.

IN LOVE

At their best, Perfectionists are faithful and committed. They value their families and are forgiving to partners who admit and honestly try to rectify their errors. At their worst, they are overly critical, dogmatic, and jealous, and they perpetually try to reform their partners.

AT WORK

- Perfectionists are detail-oriented and prefer set guidelines, scheduling, and chains of command.
- They are devoted to doing a good job for its own sake.

- Concerned more with the task than with relationships in the workplace, they will stand alone if they think others are in error or unethical. Fearful of being wrong, Perfectionists don't take risks and have trouble delegating authority to others.

- They thrive when the project or campaign is worthwhile, the leader is able and fair, and their coworkers are skilled and devoted.

MIGHT THIS BE YOUR THEME SONG?

"The Impossible Dream," from *Man of Lamanche*

5

Point Two: The Caregiver

COULD THIS BE YOU?

Imagine that the winter holidays are close at hand. You're sitting at your desk feeling swamped by your many year-end reports to be finished by December 31. You wonder if you could delegate some of the work to your assistant, but quickly reject that notion. After all, how could you ask, knowing that her husband has been sick? You wouldn't want to spoil your relationship with her. Besides, there really isn't anyone who can give those reports the same care that you do.

Your phone rings. It's your colleague from the sales department. He begs you to plan the office holiday party because, as he says, no one can do it quite like you. Feeling put upon and flattered at the same time, you accept the burdensome task. Knowing the preferences of every staff member, you spend your whole weekend planning detail upon detail of the meal, the decorations, and the entertainment.

The date arrives, and as the party progresses you scan the room, noticing everyone's feelings about how things are going. You flit from group to group, making pleasant conversation and responding to each person appropriately. You're relieved and gratified to see that everybody is having such a good time.

The next morning, again at your desk, a familiar emptiness drains your heart. You took care of everybody yesterday—everybody, that is, but yourself. To each you were the perfect host, but underneath, you wonder, who is the true you? From the time you were a child you received attention only when you were giving. Your phone rings, and you are sure that the same routine is about to start again. . . .

Caregivers are:

AT BEST	AS TENSION BUILDS	AT WORST
Nurturing	Codependent	Self-serving
Empathetic	Flattering	Manipulative
Supportive	Cloying	Guilt-instilling
Altruistic	Interfering	Smothering
Helpers	Martyrs	Victimizers

TAKING STOCK

Check the statements that best describe you in your late teens to mid-twenties.

- ☐ Being in a relationship is very important to me. When isolated, I feel as if my world might fall apart.
- ☐ I take pride in knowing others' needs without their having to ask.
- ☐ My personality tends to alter depending on whom I'm with.
- ☐ Being liked by others is very important to me.
- ☐ While I'm good at knowing the needs of others, I often don't know my own.
- ☐ I tend to separate groups of friends and associates with little connection between the different groups.
- ☐ Although I'm good at giving help, I have a hard time receiving it from others.
- ☐ I don't need others as much as they need me.
- ☐ When I was young I learned that flattery and praise are effective tools in getting others to like me.

☐ Sometimes I find it hard to relate to others except in the role of helper.

☐ I feel especially drawn to powerful people with status.

☐ I like the challenge of pursuing a difficult or even unattainable relationship. Once successful, I sometimes wonder whether I even wanted it to begin with.

☐ I can feel resentful and smothered when I'm expected to be a constant helper.

☐ When not helping others, I have a hard time knowing who I am.

☐ I have a hard time saying "no."

BLESSINGS OF BEING A CAREGIVER

• I am caring, helpful, and giving.

• I am attuned to the feelings, needs, and wants of others.

• I am friendly and sociable, and I can lift others when they feel low.

DIFFICULTIES OF BEING A CAREGIVER

• Being alone can be difficult for me.

• I can be manipulative and controlling through my helpfulness.

• When I don't receive love and appreciation for my efforts, I can play the martyr and can become vengeful.

WINGS

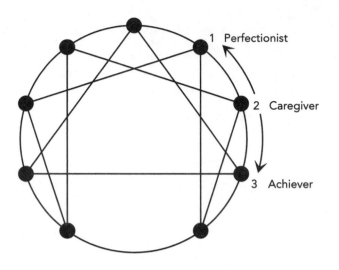

The wings of type 2 are 1 and 3

Your core personality type can be influenced by the points adjacent to yours. Usually one of the wings is stronger and can have a distinct effect on your personality.

Caregivers with a pronounced One (Perfectionist) wing can seem more circumspect and conscience-bound. Principled and altruistic, they can at times become rigid and moralizing.

Caregivers with a pronounced Three (Achiever) wing can seem more charming and personable. Gregarious and self-confident, they can also be self-servingly exploitative, with an exaggerated sense of personal entitlement.

ARROWS

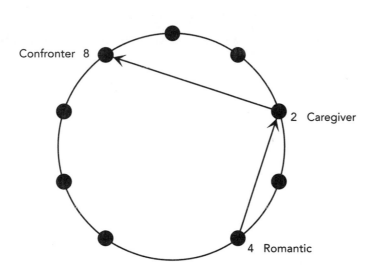

When feeling secure, Caregivers can display tendencies of the Four (Romantic).

Positive Traits

• You become more self-reflective, in touch with all of your feelings—even the negative ones.
• You are more authentic and accepting of yourself.
• You are more creative and can give more deeply of yourself.

Negative Trait

• You can become preoccupied with your own wants, and petulant when others don't acknowledge your uniqueness.

When under stress, Caregivers move towards Eight (Confronter).

Negative Traits

- You can become domineering and aggressive.
- When your efforts go unappreciated, you can be vengeful and even destructive.
- You can feel justified in being boastful and acting the bully toward others.

Positive Trait

- You can become more straightforward, practical, and goal-oriented.

AS A CHILD

- You were rewarded for being warm, engaging, helpful, amusing, and/or flattering.
- Anticipating and then fulfilling the needs of others earned you affection and approval.
- Rarely were your needs taken into account. When you asserted them, you might have been made to feel selfish.
- You learned to alter yourself to meet the expectations of others at the expense of your true self.
- You were appreciated when you were caring and sympathetic.

IN LOVE

At their best, Caregivers are loving, caring, giving, fun, and dedicated to helping their partners fulfill their noblest traits. At their worst, they are indirect, controlling, manipulative, and cloying, and they see themselves as being indispensable to their partners' lives.

AT WORK

- Caregivers are "people people" who recognize the needs of supervisors, coworkers, customers and clients—and then work tenaciously to fulfill them.

- Often preferring support positions, Caregivers are reliable, encouraging, and helpful. They gain status and influence because powerful people come to depend on them.

- Caregivers wish to be appreciated and recognized for the essential role they've played in the success of those they have helped. At times their help can come with a host of underlying demands and a desire to control others "for their own good."

MIGHT THIS BE YOUR THEME SONG?

"Bridge Over Troubled Water," by Simon & Garfunkel

6

Point Three: The Achiever

COULD THIS BE YOU?

You have been invited to attend a gala cocktail reception sponsored by your fraternal order. As you enter the large hall you notice that it is packed with people you absolutely must impress. Fellow members are all potential customers or sources of referral. You feel a deep need to interact with each of them before they leave. After all, you never know who will feel slighted and think less of you if you don't at least say hello.

You move from conversation to conversation, trying to appear interested and engaged. Yet, all the while your mind is strategically plotting your next move—monitoring, listening, watching, setting up your next conversation.

A good friend approaches and begins to share a painful experience. As he pours out his heart you overhear a disparaging remark made from the group to your right. Could it be about you? Your entire attention shifts while your friend continues to share his heart-rending tale. You feel compelled to refute this perceived insult but don't want your friend to think that you're heartless. Smoothly, you pawn him off on a more sympathetic ear while your mind turns completely to the task of damage control.

Before leaving the gala, you seek some positive affirmation from a known admirer. On arriving home, you're greeted by your spouse and children, each brimming with something to tell you. Your pretense at sharing their enthusiasm almost turns to irritation. How can they expect you to be available to them when you have more important things to think about? Still caught in your anxiety over the perceived criticism, you begin to consider your options and strategies for the next day. . . .

Achievers are:

AT BEST	AS TENSION BUILDS	AT WORST
Energetic	Driven	Workaholic
Self-assured	Self-promoting	Condescending
Efficient	Expedient	Devious
Multifaceted	Chameleon-like	Pretentious
Human paragons	Slick	Hollow

TAKING STOCK

Check the statements that best describe you in your late teens to mid-twenties.

☐ It's very important for me to appear successful. If not, I feel as if my world might fall apart.

☐ If I'm not good at something, I tend not to do it, even if it's just a game.

☐ More often than not, I will speak of my defeats as partial victories or as springboards to future success.

☐ Getting the job done can be more important to me than almost anything—even, at times, my relationships.

☐ I like to accomplish as much as I can, even if it means cutting a few corners.

☐ If it works, use it.

☐ Status, recognition, and financial security are important and should be earned.

☐ When things go badly, I have been known to blame circumstances or even other people for the problem.

☐ Even though I am quite concerned about what other people think of me, I have trouble getting close to others.

☐ I have a wide variety of interests, although I don't delve into many very deeply.

☐ I can feel as if I have a little taskmaster sitting on my shoulder, constantly telling me to do more.

☐ Even when another person is doing something well, I often think I could do it better. Some people find me arrogant and grandiose.

☐ I like to be noticed and am often left in charge.

☐ How I present myself usually depends on the expectations and values of those whom I am with. Some people think I'm slick or even deceptive. I just see it as doing what's appropriate for the circumstances.

☐ I always try to put my best foot forward.

BLESSINGS OF BEING AN ACHIEVER

• I am hardworking and willing to do everything necessary to get the job done.

• I can accomplish a great deal in a very short time.

• I am upbeat and enthusiastic, and I have a great variety of interests.

DIFFICULTIES OF BEING AN ACHIEVER

• I am pompous at times and will occasionally overstate my qualifications and achievements to appear impressive.

• I can move too quickly through projects without giving enough thought to potential drawbacks, the group process, or the feelings of others.

• My flurry of activity often masks my own discomfort with intimacy or my own feelings. Doing comes easily. Being or being with is much harder.

WINGS

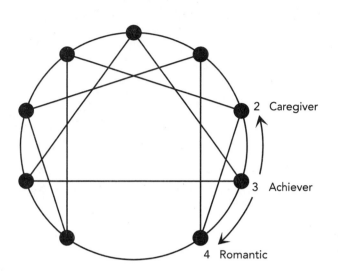

The wings of type 3 and 2 and 4

Your core personality type can be influenced by the points adjacent to yours. Usually one of the wings is stronger and can have a distinct effect on your personality.

Achievers with a pronounced Two (Caregiver) wing can appear more gregarious and emotionally demonstrative. While they can be charming, responsive, and encouraging, at times they can become preoccupied with gaining attention and can feign concern and sincerity when they wish to impress others.

Achievers with a pronounced Four (Romantic) wing can seem goal-oriented and subdued. Self-confident, introspective, and concerned with mastering their chosen field, they can also be moody, pretentious, and caught between self-aggrandizement and self-doubt.

ARROWS

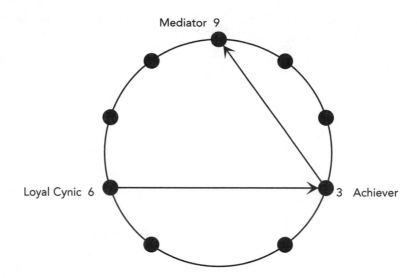

When feeling secure, Achievers can display tendencies of the Six (Loyal Cynic).

Positive Traits

- You become more supportive of others and less concerned with your own prestige.
- You feel empowered to commit yourself to causes beyond your own personal concerns.
- You more honestly examine your feelings and open up to others.

Negative Trait

- You can become more dependent on others and fear their rejection.

When under stress, Achievers move towards Nine (Mediator).

Negative Traits

- You can lose focus, becoming disinterested and sluggish.
- You might avoid reality by fantasizing or anesthetizing yourself with TV, novels, food, or substance abuse.
- You can procrastinate and stubbornly refuse to consider problems.

Positive Trait

- Rather than being as goal-driven as usual, you can enjoy tranquility and gain a wider perspective on deeper issues.

AS A CHILD

- Your parents prized good grades and achievements, not just you for being who you were.
- Your feelings were ignored or even belittled.
- You were involved in a wide variety of activities.
- You found that a good way to get what you wanted was to become what others wanted you to be.
- You were able to out-achieve others through efficiency, organization, dedication, and perseverance.

IN LOVE

At their best, Achievers are supportive, good providers, and encouraging of their partners. At their worst, they falsely play the role of being loving and avoid intimacy through immersion in work.

AT WORK

- Achievers are productive and efficient.
- They function best in environments with clearly delineated paths for promotion, constructive feedback, recognition, and plenty of room for advancement.
- While Achievers can inspire their coworkers to even greater achievement, they can also undermine team morale by striving to gain personal recognition. They can ignore the feelings of others and cast blame or even jump ship when a project begins to falter.

MIGHT THIS BE YOUR THEME SONG?

"I Can't Get Next to You," by the Temptations

7

Point Four: The Romantic

COULD THIS BE YOU?

It is a dark winter night. As you sit by yourself in front of the fire you feel lonely, wishing someone was there to hold you. You wonder if anyone could possibly understand your feelings. If only there was someone who would listen, who could share your emotions, who feels as deeply as you do. Your mind turns to a special love, recalling the last time you were together. A sweet, sad ache throbs in your heart as you savor how much you miss that love.

The phone rings, shattering your melancholy. You hear the voice of your beloved from long ago. "Honey, I'm coming to town next week, and I can't wait to see you. It's been too long. I don't know how we ever drifted apart."

Your veil of sadness begins to lift. Yearning and anticipation fill each day as you wait for this loving, fulfilling, sure-to-be-perfect encounter. The day arrives, the doorbell rings, and there stands your special someone. You embrace with a kiss and a smile. You pour out your hearts to each other, sharing secrets and intimacies. As the day continues, familiar twinges of dissatisfaction start to emerge. "If only my beloved were more caring, more in touch, more tender, more . . ."

As your shared day draws to a close you look wistfully into the fireplace, feeling distant even as you cuddle.

"Honey, what is it?"

"I know it's strange, but I miss you already."

"Please don't miss me yet. I'm still here."

And although you recognize that this is true, you can't help but feel a little empty, alone once again. . . .

Romantics are:

AT BEST	AS TENSION BUILDS	AT WORST
Self-aware	Overly Sensitive	Tormented
Authentic	Dramatic	Eccentric
Passionate	Moody	Depressed
Distinctive	Aloof	Alienated
Caring	Deprived	Abandoned

TAKING STOCK

Check the statements that best describe you in your late teens to mid-twenties.

☐ Depth of feeling is very important to me. Without intense experience I feel as if my world might fall apart.

☐ I often feel as if something is missing from my life.

☐ When things go wrong, I tend to feel that the flaw is in me, rather than merely in my actions.

☐ A thin line of melancholy seems to run through my life. Rarely, if ever, does it go away.

☐ I can be envious of others, wondering if they are entitled to some kind of fulfillment that is denied me.

☐ I love being surrounded by beauty.

☐ I think of myself as distinctive and special.

☐ Honesty and authenticity are of prime importance to me.

☐ I often yearn for what was or what is yet to be. This makes it tough to enjoy what I have in the present.

☐ Many times I feel alone, like an outsider.

☐ I can be helpful to others when they experience crisis and emotional distress.

☐ I measure success not by the quantity but by the depth and originality of my work.

☐ I am sensitive and emotional. When depressed I find it very hard to get on with my life.

☐ More than anything else, I want to be understood.

BLESSINGS OF BEING A ROMANTIC

- I live life with intensity and passion.
- I am intuitive, bringing creativity and emotional depth to my work.
- I always try to be authentic, and I won't abide insincerity and falsehood.

DIFFICULTIES OF BEING A ROMANTIC

- My longing for what was or what could be can blind me to the blessings of what is.
- At times I can be paralyzed by depression or sorrow.
- Others can think of me as overly dramatic, self-absorbed and perpetually unsatisfied.

WINGS

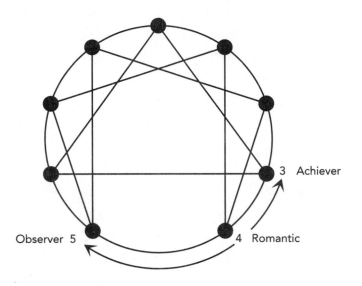

The wings of type 4 are 3 and 5

Your core personality type can be influenced by the points adjacent to yours. Usually one of the wings is stronger and can have a distinct effect on your personality.

Romantics with a pronounced Three (Achiever) wing appear more goal-oriented and more aware of interpersonal dynamics. Energetic and motivated to make their own distinctive contributions, they can be self-contemptuous and hurtful in their envy, and they can take advantage of situations and others.

Romantics with a pronounced Five (Observer) wing seem more intense, emotionally deep, and retiring. Insightful, sensitive, and creative, at times they can become pessimistic, alienated from others, and tortured by inner doubts.

ARROWS

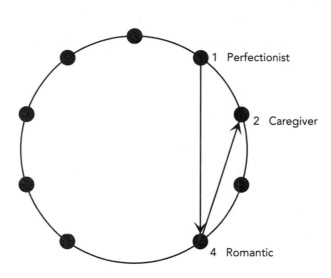

When feeling secure, Romantics can display tendencies of the One (Perfectionist).

Positive Traits

- You become more objective in your judgment, relying less on your feelings.
- You can act on principle and become less self-involved.
- Rather than being oppositional and disregarding ordinary norms, you begin to recognize the validity of limits and acting with disciplined restraint.

Negative Trait

- You can become both overly idealistic and overly critical.

When under stress, Romantics move towards Two (Caregiver).

Negative Traits

- You can become cloying and manipulative.
- You can seek to escape from confronting your own problems by trying to help others.
- You can become overly concerned that others recognize every little thing you do for them as special.

Positive Trait

- You can move beyond self-absorption to true empathy and service to others.

AS A CHILD

- You felt abandoned or left behind.
- You gained attention by being "special."
- Death, divorce, emotional withdrawal, moving, or some other loss shattered the "original rightness" of your world.
- You felt the shame of being an outsider, and you often felt inferior to others.
- Your moods shifted as one (or both) of your parents shifted between concern and withdrawal, being caring and then wounding.

IN LOVE

At their best, Romantics are passionate, supportive, attuned to beauty and nuance, and reliable during crisis and loss. At their worst, they are envious and fault-finding, and they keep their partners on an endless roller coaster by drawing them near and then pulling away.

AT WORK

- Romantics value creativity, depth, and vision in their work.
- They are devoted to process and finding their own way. Rarely will they accept things on another's authority or say-so.
- Romantics thrive in environments in which their uniqueness is recognized. But in the face of being overwhelmed by emotions, they need to strive toward objectivity, perseverance, and disciplined effort.

MIGHT THIS BE YOUR THEME SONG?

"So Far Away," by Carole King

8

Point Five: The Observer

COULD THIS BE YOU?

You are on your way to the annual conference of your professional association. The overall theme is one that has interested you for years. To prepare, you've reviewed your books and journals on the topic and surfed the relevant sites on the Web. After all, you can never have too much knowledge or be too prepared.

As you pick up your folder at the registration desk you glance at the conference schedule. "Oh, no!" you think to yourself. Tonight's opening event is a cocktail reception aimed at giving the participants a chance to get acquainted. Knowing that you and large gatherings of strangers go together as well as ice cream and enchiladas, you give serious thought to staying in your room. But in the end, you feel obligated to attend for a short while.

As you enter the hall you look around for the exits as well as for any big potted plant to serve as cover. You feel as if your consciousness has detached itself from your body and is now hovering around the ceiling, observing the goings-on. Notice the refreshments and the drinks. Notice the décor and the table placement. Notice the raucous group to your right—too loud and overbearing—so avoid them. Notice the time—can you leave yet?

Realizing that you've hardly breathed since you walked in, you make eye contact with another participant. Time to summon up courage, go over, and start a conversation. "What do you think about . . ." you begin. Your conversation partner responds in kind. All right—an intellectual discussion. Maybe this party isn't so bad. In fact, maybe this person now talking to me isn't so bad either, though you could never just come out and say that.

Later, in the privacy of your room, you review the evening's events, analyzing what you might feel about your conversation partner and looking forward to what you might learn the next day. . . .

Observers are:

AT BEST	AS TENSION BUILDS	AT WORST
Insightful	Analytical	Abstract
Probing	Detached	Reclusive
Self-sufficient	Withholding	Miserly
Sagely	Pedantic	Out of touch
Scholarly	Aloof	Rejecting social contact

TAKING STOCK

Check the statements that best describe you in your late teens to mid-twenties.

☐ Privacy is very important to me. Without sufficient time alone, I feel as if my world might fall apart.

☐ I love to investigate different areas of knowledge.

☐ No matter how much I study, I rarely feel as if I know enough about the topic I am exploring.

☐ I often feel uncomfortable when others get all "gooey" and emotional.

☐ I'd rather make do with less than surrender my independence.

☐ Knowledge is power.

☐ My space and belongings are almost sacred to me. If others disturb them I feel violated.

☐ If I were to become famous, it would be in a way that would let people know my name and work but not me—like being an author or a theorist.

☐ Sometimes it's hard for me to complete projects because there always seems to be something more I need to prepare.

☐ I am much more at home in my head than in my heart.

☐ I do best in public situations when I know in advance what is expected of me and how long the event will take.

☐ Others see me as detached or unemotional. I disagree: I simply prefer to be alone when processing my feelings.

☐ I love mastering large systems of knowledge, like sociology or mathematics, that uncover patterns of coherence and meaning in our world.

☐ I'm not much of a joiner. I find interest groups more attractive than social clubs, particularly when I can contribute some special expertise.

☐ On the whole, the world is an intrusive place.

BLESSINGS OF BEING AN OBSERVER

• I love to probe, explore, and learn.

• I am independent and self-sufficient.

• I am at my best when I can share my insights and discoveries with others.

DIFFICULTIES OF BEING AN OBSERVER

• Social interactions are often very uncomfortable for me.

• I can become so engrossed in my own thoughts that I lose touch with reality.

• Giving to others of my time, space, or resources is not easy for me.

WINGS

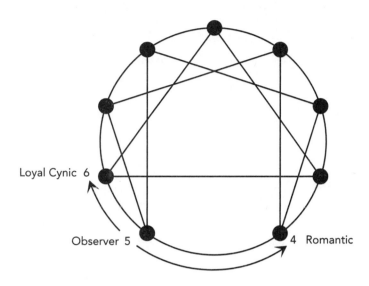

The wings of type 5 are 4 and 6

Your core personality type can be influenced by the points adjacent to yours. Usually one of the wings is stronger and can have a distinct effect on your personality.

Observers with a pronounced Four (Romantic) wing can seem imaginative and emotional. Intuitive, innovative, and able to see beauty in the patterns of reality, they can have trouble sustaining projects, working with others, and being caught in their own dark, terrifying fantasies.

Observers with a pronounced Six (Loyal Cynic) wing can appear more outgoing and analytical. Probing, disciplined, and able to draw important conclusions from a wide range of data, they can be socially marginal and antagonistic, and they can bury themselves in intellectual tasks rather than face their problems.

ARROWS

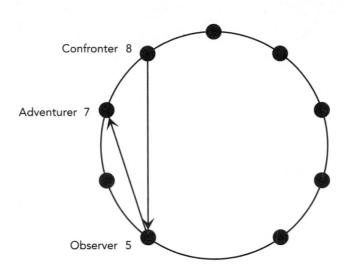

When feeling secure, Observers can display tendencies of the Eight (Confronter).

Positive Traits

- You become more outgoing and assertive.
- You can translate your theories and concepts into actions.
- Because you are more confident and trusting, you can step into positions of leadership.

Negative Trait

- You may become antagonistic, cruelly using your knowledge to retain authority and to gain revenge.

When under stress, Observers move towards Seven (Adventurer).

Negative Traits

- You can become restless, looking unsuccessfully for fulfillment in an ever-changing variety of topics and interests.

- You get easily distracted and find it hard to stay on task.

- You can lose control, become increasingly impatient, and adopt a "Who cares?" attitude.

Positive Trait

- You can become more playful, imaginative, and spontaneous.

AS A CHILD

- Your parents were invasive, not respecting your boundaries or space.

- You did well in school and were appreciated for your grades and study habits.

- You experienced your parents as withdrawn and emotionally stingy, so you became withdrawn and stingy toward yourself and others.

- Your thoughts and fantasies seemed more compelling and secure than what was going on in reality.

- Since knowledge is power, it was safer not to let others know what you were thinking.

IN LOVE

At their best, Observers make enduring commitments, connect on a variety of levels, and express their affection in non-verbal ways. At their worst, they can be cold and withdrawn, requiring their partners to take all initiative in the relationship.

AT WORK

- Observers like to work independently, free from intrusion and excessive or intense contact.

- They like their information presented in a systematic and thoughtful way. They have very little tolerance for sloppy thinking.

- They are analytical, objective in their decision-making, and interested in knowing the underlying theories of what they investigate.

MIGHT THIS BE YOUR THEME SONG?

"I Am a Rock," by Simon & Garfunkel

9

Point Six: The Loyal Cynic

COULD THIS BE YOU?

It's a stormy evening, and you're alone on a deserted road. Your tire has just gone flat, and you're sure that you just missed your turnoff. You pull off the road and remember that you passed a gas station about a mile back. Should you go for help, or is it safer to just stay where you are? As you open the car door you hear the cracking of branches. Is someone or some creature out there? Quickly you shut the door. It's cold, but if you start the engine to turn on the heat—what about the fumes? That could be just as dangerous.

You leave the car and walk back toward the gas station. A million thoughts fly through your head. Will the station be open? If so, will they have the right tire or be able to fix the flat? Will they be courteous, be rude, or even refuse to help?

You reach the station and open the door. For reasons that may exist only in your mind, you speak belligerently to the attendant before he can even say hello. . . .

Loyal Cynics are:

AT BEST	AS TENSION BUILDS	AT WORST
Sensible	Anxious	Insecure
Cautious	Suspicious	Catastrophizing
Respectful	Traditional	Dogmatic
Questioning	Oppositional	Bullying
Determined	Rigid	Authoritarian

TAKING STOCK

Check the statements that best describe you in your late teens to mid-twenties.

☐ Safety is very important to me. When I am not vigilant, I feel as if my world might fall apart.

☐ Loyalty, sacrifice, and teamwork are traits I try to embody in my life.

☐ People say that I am oppositional and have a doubting mind.

☐ I am usually suspicious of those in authority until they prove themselves trustworthy.

☐ While others might be gullible, I can smell a phony a hundred yards away.

☐ I have a hard time being in the spotlight because I wonder whether others will express their approval or just criticize me.

☐ Sometimes I deal with my fears by taking flight. At other times, I rush headlong into risky situations to prove that I'm not afraid.

☐ In a dispute I often take the side of the underdog.

☐ I have been known to procrastinate. I can actually do my best work with my back against the wall.

☐ My mind just naturally seems to scan wherever I find myself, searching for potential danger and harm.

☐ Although I yearn for approval, dealing with success and recognition doesn't come easily to me.

☐ I tend to look for hidden meanings and implications in the statements of others.

☐ I see the dark clouds behind every silver lining.

☐ I can be quite ambivalent when relating to authority, hoping that the leader is competent and worthy while always checking for weakness and hidden agendas.

☐ I am a hard worker who likes it best when the guidelines are clear. I have little tolerance for slackers and for behavior I consider deviant.

BLESSINGS OF BEING A LOYAL CYNIC

- I am diligent and faithful.
- I can see through pretense and fraud.
- I will make sacrifices for the good of the team and defend those who are weak.

DIFFICULTIES OF BEING A LOYAL CYNIC

- I can become paralyzed by my own doubts.
- At times I project my fears upon others, ascribing harmful motives that aren't really there.
- When facing fear I can be unduly cautious or unduly reckless.

WINGS

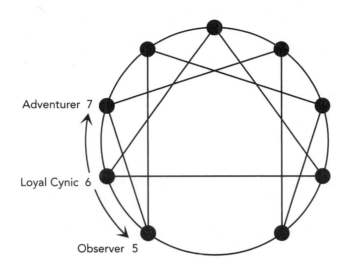

Adventurer 7

Loyal Cynic 6

Observer 5

The wings of type 6 are 5 and 7

Your core personality type can be influenced by the points adjacent to yours. Usually one of the wings is stronger and can have a distinct effect on your personality.

Loyal Cynics with a pronounced Five (Observer) wing can seem more intense, disciplined, and dedicated to their ethical and social beliefs. Champions of the weak and excellent troubleshooters, they can become competitive, secretive, and obsessive about maintaining security.

Loyal Cynics with a pronounced Seven (Adventurer) wing can be more sociable, spontaneous, humorous, and eager to gain the approval of others. Friendly and helpful, with a wide range of interests, they can become anxious and indecisive, and blame others for their woes.

ARROWS

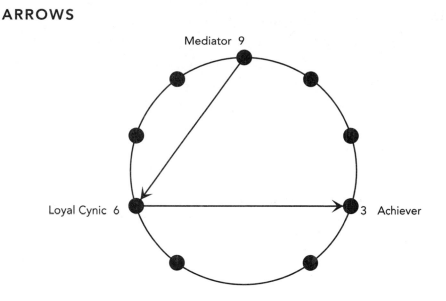

When feeling secure, Loyal Cynics can display tendencies of the Nine (Mediator).

Positive Traits
- You feel more at peace and personally secure.
- You are more supportive of others and open to their views.
- You become more optimistic and trusting.

Negative Trait
- You may find yourself becoming distracted and more of a procrastinator.

When under stress, Loyal Cynics move towards Three (Achiever).

Negative Traits

- As a way of suppressing your fears, you become very task-oriented.
- Questions about how others perceive you become overly important as you try to avoid rejection.
- You can become self-promoting and demeaning of others.

Positive Trait

- Instead of focusing on your fears, you focus more easily on what you can accomplish.

AS A CHILD

- You were rewarded for being diligent and following the rules.
- You picked up on one of your parents' fears of the outside world.
- Because of the capricious way a parent exercised authority, you began to doubt your natural responses and tried to figure out how you might please that parent.
- To defend your sense of self from the intrusiveness or unpredictability of those with power, you began to rebel.
- You learned that this world was a dangerous place, but there could be safety in following the rules.

IN LOVE

At their best, Loyal Cynics can be cheerful, devoted, and supportive of their partners, even in the most difficult of situations. At their worst, they become secretive and provocative, projecting their own faults onto their partners and justifying their own hurtfulness by claiming that they are the real victims.

AT WORK

- Loyal Cynics are focused, dependable, and good with details.
- They are able to spot frauds, weaknesses in arguments, and the potential land mines that can sabotage a project.
- Because of their suspicious nature and vigilance, Loyal Cynics can become preoccupied with questions of authority and procrastinate rather than take the risks needed to get things done.

MIGHT THIS BE YOUR THEME SONG?

"Honesty," by Billy Joel

10

Point Seven: The Adventurer

COULD THIS BE YOU?

You arise in the morning full of enthusiasm, happy to meet the new day. Imagine—it's the weekend, and you can do whatever you want! You stretch your arms and legs and then steal a glance at the alarm clock. Wow, it's 9:45 A.M., and you just remember that you have an appointment to have your hair cut at 11:15. Damn, right in the middle of this glorious day! Well, it might not be so bad. Your favorite newsstand is right around the corner, and this month's magazines should have just arrived. A new hairstyle, a little browsing—this could be okay.

Or maybe not. While pulling on your clothes you remember that you've promised to have coffee with a friend at about the same time on the other side of town. You've rescheduled this date twice and just hate to put it off again. But if you cancel with the hairstylist, you'll have to pay anyway, and the scalp massage that comes with the shampoo is too good to miss.

Suddenly you get a flash. You call your friend, "Why don't we do dinner and a concert tonight?"

"No," comes the irritated response, "I can't make it then."

You quickly say goodbye, deciding to call later on and send a card to patch things up. Now it's off to the hairstylist for that yummy scalp massage, your magazines, and then maybe off to that dinner and a concert if you choose. The only problem with days like this is that they're only twenty-four hours long. . . .

Adventurers are:

AT BEST	AS TENSION BUILDS	AT WORST
Optimistic	Impractical	Unrealistic
Spontaneous	Impulsive	Irresponsible
Fun-loving	Indulgent	Narcissistic
Visionary	Fantasizing	Escapist
Enthusiastic	Excitable	Infantile

TAKING STOCK

Check the statements that best describe you in your late teens to mid-twenties.

☐ It's very important to me to have my options open at all times. When I'm restricted, I feel as if my world might fall apart.

☐ I am a very upbeat person.

☐ I like to be surrounded with high-energy people like myself who share similar interests.

☐ Although I can be good at helping others, I find emotionally needy people much too draining.

☐ I have a wide variety of interests and like to sample a lot of different things.

☐ I have an ability to find connections among various subjects in ways that others usually don't.

☐ I rarely see setbacks as crushing defeats. My motto is "If confronted with a pile of manure, start digging—there must be a pony in there somewhere."

☐ While others find me likeable, I'm not always good at keeping appointments or commitments.

☐ I live life as an adventure.

☐ I am resilient and seem to recover from setbacks faster than others.

☐ I try to avoid painful situations whenever possible.

☐ I am outgoing and friendly, but many of my relationships remain at the surface level.

☐ I enjoy having fun, but in my quest for adventure I sometimes overlook potential dangers that lurk beneath the surface.

☐ I love envisioning new ideas, but I am less enamored with the "grunt work" needed to make them happen.

☐ Life should be colorful and lived vibrantly.

BLESSINGS OF BEING AN ADVENTURER

- I am outgoing and entertaining.
- I am creative and see endless realms of new possibilities.
- I value and enjoy life.

DIFFICULTIES OF BEING AN ADVENTURER

- I have problems with limits and commitments.
- I have little tolerance for emotionally demanding people or situations.
- I get bored easily and can abandon a task before completion to go on to something else that seems more exciting.

WINGS

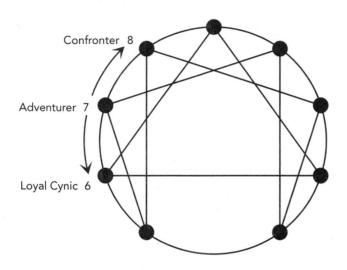

The wings of type 7 are 6 and 8

Your core personality type can be influenced by the points adjacent to yours. Usually one of the wings is stronger and can have a distinct effect on your personality.

Adventurers with a pronounced Six (Loyal Cynic) wing seem more outgoing, playful, and able to inspire others with their joy. Entertaining, generous, and spunky, they move quickly in and out of relationships, become insecure about whether to stay or move on, and overly solicit the help of others to solve their problems.

Adventurers with a pronounced Eight (Confronter) wing can seem more goal-oriented, hardworking, realistic, and persevering. Confident, assertive, and daring, they can be direct to the point of rudeness, and they disregard both the bounds of propriety and the sensitivities of others while seeking the rush that comes from living dangerously.

ARROWS

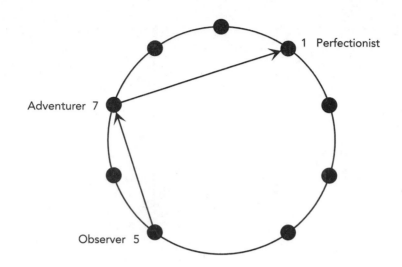

When feeling secure, Adventurers can display tendencies of the Five (Observer).

Positive Traits

- You become comfortable with solitude.
- You are more interested in the underlying meaning of your experiences.
- Your appreciation of life takes on a sense of awe at the wonder of existence.

Negative Trait

- You may retreat from others and become even more acquisitive of experiences and things.

When under stress, Adventurers move towards One (Perfectionist).

Negative Traits

- You may become more rigid and impatient.
- Rather than finding joy in your surroundings, you can be more critical, searching out the least little flaws.
- You may feel a need to impose limits on yourself and then chafe at these boundaries, becoming frustrated when you overstep them.

Positive Trait

- Rather than just doing what feels good, you can be moved to do what is right, and in an ordered, systematic manner.

AS A CHILD

- You were brought up in a happy home.
- You were rewarded for being joyous and happy.
- When you experienced hurt and pain, you would block out the experience or reframe it as something positive.
- You were treated like someone special who was entitled to good things.
- You loved to daydream about adventure, often finding the planning more fun than the actual doing.

IN LOVE

At their best, Adventurers are playful, interesting, and able to lift their partners' spirits when things are low. At their worst, they have trouble with commitment and seek escape if their partners become too emotionally needy or depressed.

AT WORK

- Adventurers are creative and have the ability to approach challenges in innovative ways.
- They can be quite inspirational and can help to motivate their team.
- Because of their problem with commitment, Adventurers are not always great on details and follow-through.

MIGHT THIS BE YOUR THEME SONG?

"L'Chayim (To Life)," from *Fiddler on the Roof*

11

Point Eight: The Confronter

COULD THIS BE YOU?

Your world was initially filled with toys and treats, with smiles and trust in everyone. Then came the taunts and the fighting, the hurtful words and acts at home, the bullies on the playground. The world seemed hostile, so you had to choose: be vulnerable and cease to be, or be powerful and seize control. So you hid your innocence and learned that if you asserted yourself and challenged others you often got your way.

The world can be unjust, and you need to set things right. Like that time in the schoolyard when the older kids started to tease the kid on crutches. "Gimp!" they cried, pushing her as the tears streamed helplessly down her face. You felt your body tense as the energy flowed through you. Overwhelmed by the unfairness of that girl's plight, you were blind to everything else—including the number and size of the bullies. Oblivious to fear and fueled by outrage, you heard your voice thunder at the group as you rushed them head on.

"No one will get away with this—not while I'm around!"

Waking from your reverie, you see a coworker coming toward your desk. He wants to share a concern with you, but the more he tries to explain his side, the angrier you become. "Why is he always putting me down?" you think as you respond to your colleague in a voice just louder than his. Your energy rises in your body, and your voice seems to grow until it's as if you fill the entire room. You peer down at your puny antagonist, summoning whatever physical and verbal expressions you need to ensure that no one will ever get the better of you. . . .

Confronters are:

AT BEST	AS TENSION BUILDS	AT WORST
Assertive	Belligerent	Combative
Just	Domineering	Vengeful
Forceful	Intimidating	Bullying
Protective	Possessive	Dictatorial
Courageous	Willful	Macho

TAKING STOCK

Check the statements that best describe you in your late teens to mid-twenties.

☐ Being in control is very important to me. When I'm vulnerable, I feel as if my world might fall apart.

☐ I want to be recognized as an effective, competent person.

☐ The world can be unfair, and at times I feel compelled to right those wrongs.

☐ If you push me, know that I'm going to push back.

☐ I hate "whiners" but will always try to help those in real need, particularly when they're also willing to help themselves.

☐ If you have bad news, tell me the truth. I have little tolerance for those who dissemble.

☐ Be it food, drink, partying, or work, I have a tendency to go to excess.

☐ While most people try to avoid conflict, I find confrontation clarifying. That way I can tell who is being honest and who isn't.

☐ While it doesn't seem that way to me, others tell me that I'm too loud, too pushy, too big—in short, just too much.

☐ Loyalty is very important to me. My true friends stand by me through the good and the bad. I would never consider deserting them.

☐ As much as I prefer not to be, I am easily provoked. Sometimes all it takes is a stray word or a skewed glance to set me off.

☐ I like to stir things up when times seem dull or people are getting complacent.

☐ I have a soft spot for children, small animals, and others who are truly weak. Anyone who tries to hurt them will have to answer to me.

☐ Rarely do I let anyone get the best of me. It might seem vengeful, but I'll keep the "game" going until I prevail.

☐ Beneath my big persona I have feelings like everyone else. It's just that I won't display my sensitivities to anyone except those few whom I know I can trust.

BLESSINGS OF BEING A CONFRONTER

• I am faithful and strong.
• I am capable of achieving difficult tasks against overwhelming odds.
• I have a strong sense of integrity and justice.

DIFFICULTIES OF BEING A CONFRONTER

• I can be intimidating and insensitive to the feelings of others.
• I can be excessive and not realize when it's time to stop.
• I am easily insulted and, at times, show a vengeful streak.

WINGS

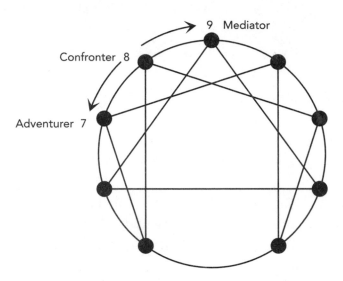

The wings of type 8 are 7 and 9

Your core personality type can be influenced by the points adjacent to yours. Usually one of the wings is stronger and can have a distinct effect on your personality.

Confronters with a pronounced Seven (Adventurers) wing can seem more outgoing, brusque, and assertive. Energetic, charismatic, and generous, they can become intimidating, manipulative, impulsive, and given to exaggeration.

Confronters with a pronounced Nine (Mediator) wing can, at times, appear more tranquil, receptive, and reserved. Family-oriented, quietly forceful, and in constant pursuit of their objectives, they can seem merciless and uncaring, and exhibit a pronounced separation between their belligerent and accommodating sides.

ARROWS

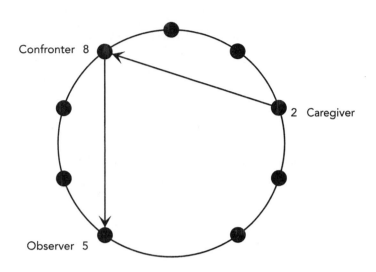

When feeling secure, Confronters can display tendencies of the Two (Caregiver).

Positive Traits

- You feel more sympathy and concern for others.
- You become more comfortable with your feelings and vulnerabilities.
- You act more humbly and put the interests of others ahead of your need for control.

Negative Trait

- You may manipulate others into needing you to reinforce your own sense of power.

When under stress, Confronters move towards Five (Observer).

Negative Traits

- You may retreat from others and become less communicative.
- To maintain power you may become stealthlike, keeping your own counsel and then striking when least expected.
- You may become more contemptuous of those less intelligent or powerful than yourself.

Positive Trait

- You act less impulsively and with more forethought.

AS A CHILD

- You were rewarded for being powerful and taking charge.
- You learned that nice guys finish last.
- You witnessed a lot of conflict at home.
- The world seemed to be unjust and dangerous, so you decided to follow your own rules and protect yourself.
- You were energetic and enjoyed feeling strong and in charge. When you challenged or threatened people, they usually backed down and let you have what you wanted.

IN LOVE

At their best, Confronters are protective, loyal, and adventurous. At their worst, they are controlling, have a hard time surrendering to intimacy, and will constantly test their partners' resolve.

AT WORK

- Confronters are thick-skinned and strong-willed leaders who get things done.
- They enjoy challenges and through force of personality are able to enlist others in their plans.
- They can be very effective entrepreneurs. However, since they usually don't work and play well with others, they lead by decree and have a hard time being in a collaborative or subordinate role.

MIGHT THIS BE YOUR THEME SONG?

"My Way," by Frank Sinatra

12
Point Nine: The Mediator

COULD THIS BE YOU?

You've been invited to lunch with a group of old friends. The restaurant they've chosen overlooks a beautiful garden. As you walk to the restaurant you see the various shades of flowers, the young mothers pushing their strollers along the path, the elderly gentlemen sitting on the park benches. You wonder whether the lady you see with the convertible remembers that she left the top down. Inside the restaurant you experience sensory overload—the voices, the aromas, the décor. You see the window treatments, the ring on the barman's hand, and the expression on the server's face.

Oh my lord! Everyone has already been seated, and you're still standing there. You take the only remaining seat and peer out the large picture window at the flowers. You overhear the conversation to your left while smelling the cigarette smoke wafting over from the smoking section. You look over the menu and feel paralyzed by the number of choices available. One by one, you begin to eliminate what you don't want until you get down to five appetizing selections. As you compare costs and fat content, and imagine the taste of each, two of your party begin to debate whether to order an entrée that the chef will prepare for a minimum of three people. As the discussion heats up, you begin to feel unsettled, so you offer to be the third. The waiter takes your orders, and as he walks away it occurs to you that what you really wanted was the Caesar salad.

Throughout lunch, your mind is drawn back to the garden, the décor, and the clanging of silverware. You notice that the woman has returned to her convertible and is having trouble with the top. The waiter distributes the dessert menu, and you are overwhelmed with impressions of apple cake, rice pudding, and tarts. Since none of them seems appropriate after the lunch you've just had, you decide to treat yourself to an ice cream later on. . . .

Mediators are:

AT BEST	AS TENSION BUILDS	AT WORST
Receptive	Indecisive	Detached
Harmonious	Uncommitted	Oblivious
Serene	Low-key	Indolent
Patient	Passive-aggressive	Obstinate
Unassuming	Permissive	Appeasing

TAKING STOCK

Check the statements that best describe you in your late teens to mid-twenties.

☐ Maintaining harmony is very important to me. When caught in conflict, I feel as if my world might fall apart.

☐ I have a hard time saying "no."

☐ When I enter a room filled with strangers, I usually want to blend in.

☐ I'm good at seeing all sides of an argument.

☐ Sometimes I have difficulty staying on task. All sorts of secondary needs seem to disrupt my attention.

☐ I often have a hard time deciding what I really want.

☐ Rather than argue with someone, I let them think I agree even when I don't.

☐ Others consider me to be calm, steady, and unthreatening.

☐ From the time I was young, I felt as if my opinions were over-looked. I hate when others break in when I'm trying to make a point.

☐ I'm often good at bringing together different sides in a dispute so that things can be worked out.

☐ If you ask me nicely, I'm almost always helpful and responsive. But act as if you expect me to do something for you, and see how stubborn I can be.

☐ In intimate relationships, I have a hard time knowing where my partner leaves off and where I begin.

☐ I have been known to procrastinate before finally making up my mind.

☐ Since all points of view have some legitimacy, I wonder at times why I should even bother having one.

☐ Once I pick a course of action, I can achieve almost anything. It just takes me quite a while to determine that course.

BLESSINGS OF BEING A MEDIATOR

• I am a calm, unpretentious person.

• My broad sense of perspective allows me to see the valid points in a variety of different views.

• I have the ability to bring people together and build consensus.

DIFFICULTIES OF BEING A MEDIATOR

• I procrastinate and am often easily distracted from the task at hand.

• I can be stubborn when others want me to do something I don't want to do.

• Because I have a hard time saying no, at times I go along with the plans of others only to find myself becoming resentful later on.

WINGS

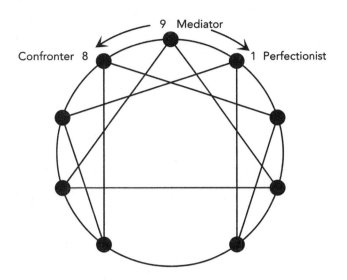

The wings of type 9 are 8 and 1

Your core personality type can be influenced by the points adjacent to yours. Usually one of the wings is stronger and can have a distinct effect on your personality.

Mediators with a pronounced Eight (Confronter) wing can be more sociable, assertive, and down-to-earth. Powerful, gracious, and possessing a good sense of humor, they can also have explosive tempers. They can swing back and forth between striving and complacency, between aggression and reconciliation.

Mediators with a pronounced One (Perfectionist) wing can be more intellectual and more emotionally and socially restrained. Idealistic, imaginative, and possessing great integrity, they can be complacent and disinterested, and can seethe over past hurts.

ARROWS

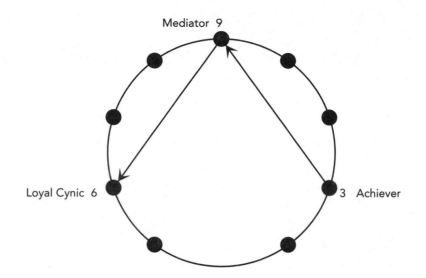

When feeling secure, Mediators can display tendencies of the Three (Achiever).

Positive Traits

- You become more assertive and willing to take the lead.
- You find that you can disagree with others and still maintain your friendships with them.
- You become more focused and able to stay on task.

Negative Trait

- You may lose yourself under a pile of work, or play a role that is at odds with who you really are.

When under stress, Mediators move towards Six (Loyal Cynic).

Negative Traits

- You may become more anxious and insecure.
- You may react more critically and defensively toward others.
- You might alternate between increasing dependence on others and outbursts of anger.

Positive Trait

- You can find the inner strength and bravery needed to stand up for yourself.

AS A CHILD

- You often felt overlooked and ignored.
- You felt torn between being the "good child" and being the "bad child," so it became easier to sit on the fence.
- Your siblings always seemed to out-perform you, causing you to feel invisible.
- You learned that if you didn't take sides, no one would be angry with you.
- Refusing to make up your mind, you enjoyed the coaxing and attention you received from others.

IN LOVE

At their best, Mediators are empathetic and supportive, and offer a calming presence in the midst of chaos. At their worst, they lose themselves in their partner's agenda, act passive-aggressively, and stay in relationships out of routine rather than conscious choice.

AT WORK

- Mediators can be counted on for their dependability and dedication.

- They are able to establish networks and bring others to consensus.

- They may have a hard time making decisions, and can lose focus on a task's essentials because of their preoccupation with trivial and inconsequential details.

MIGHT THIS BE YOUR THEME SONG?

"Fifty-Ninth Street Bridge Song," by Simon & Garfunkel

13
Your Personality Type

I hope these last chapters have given you some inkling of your personality type. If you are still having difficulty choosing between two or three possibilities, the following might be helpful:

If the points you have evaluated are adjacent, there is a good chance that one is your core point and the other is your wing. To determine which point is truly yours, it is helpful to remember the core motivations of each.

- Ones want to be correct and make things correct in this flawed world.

- Twos want to be loved for their helpfulness in this needy world.

- Threes want to be admired for their success in this image-conscious "you make it happen" world.

- Fours want to be deeply understood as special in this fractured world.

- Fives want to acquire knowledge and preserve privacy in this intrusive world.

- Sixes, by either confronting or fleeing from danger, want to insure their safety in this threatening world.

- Sevens want to explore exciting, pleasurable experiences in this all too painful, restrictive world.

- Eights want to exert and maintain control in this unjust, hostile world.

- Nines want to live in harmony in what can be an unloving, conflict-ridden world.

The circle that surrounds the nine-pointed diagram has been compared to a spectrum, with different shadings of type as it moves between the points. It is possible to be situated about dead center between two different points. If you can't decide between two adjacent types, for example Seven (Adventurer) and Eight (Confronter), ask yourself: What is my major motivation—to accumulate experience, or to accumulate power? Similarly, if stuck between Two (Caregiver) and Three (Achiever), ask yourself: Is it more important that I be loved or admired?

If the points you are evaluating are the stress and security points of each other, for example Six (Loyal Cynic) and Nine (Mediator), Two (Caregiver) and Eight (Confronter), it can be helpful to consider your current life situation. If you are now experiencing a lot of pressure, consider what you are like when things are more normal. It could be that you are now acting from your stress point rather than from your core personality. It is not unusual, particularly in ongoing pressured situations, for people to live on the connecting line between core and stress points, exhibiting characteristics of each.

If you still can't distinguish between types, note that certain points are look-alikes. They can exhibit similar behaviors but with different nuances caused by different core motivations. The following are some common look-alikes and some ways to distinguish between them.

ONE (PERFECTIONIST) LOOK-ALIKES

Ones and Threes (Achievers) are both goal-oriented and hardworking. Ones, however, are motivated by the desire to get things right according to their own inner standards; Threes are much more concerned about the opinions and acclaim of others. If choosing between these points, ask yourself: When working on a project, if no one is going to notice, do I really care if it's perfect? Also: If life is a play, do I want to be the director (Perfectionist) or the star (Achiever)?

Ones and Fours (Romantics) are both very self-critical. If deciding between these points, ask yourself: When things are going poorly ask yourself: Is it because I am *doing* something wrong (Perfectionist), or because inherently as a human being *I* am wrong (Romantic)?

Ones and Fives (Observers) are both concerned with getting complete information, and they can be procrastinators. Since Perfectionists focus on setting things right, and Observers on knowledge and privacy, ask yourself: If life were a play, would I rather be the director (Perfectionist) or the playwright (Observer)? Also: When I procrastinate, do I have trouble starting (Perfectionist) or trouble finishing (Observer)?

Ones and Sixes (Loyal Cynics) both want to get things right. When deciding between these points, ask yourself: Is the right thing determined by my own standards (Perfectionist) or by what society or my group considers right (Loyal Cynic)? Also: In the midst of planning, do I focus on fixing what is wrong (Perfectionist) or on imagining everything that could go wrong (Loyal Cynic)?

Ones and Eights (Confronters) are both interested in justice and equity. When deciding between these points, ask yourself: When things disturb me, am I more prone to let my resentment smolder under the surface (Perfectionist), or do I react immediately and possibly explode (Confronter)? Also: Is it more important to me to get things right (Perfectionist) or to be in control (Confronter)?

TWO (CAREGIVER) LOOK-ALIKES

Twos and Sixes (Loyal Cynics) are both helpful and can be quite considerate. When deciding between these points, ask yourself: Am I attracted more to difficult relationships so that I can prove my worth (Caregiver), or to comfortable relationships that make me feel secure (Loyal Cynic)?

Twos and Sevens (Adventurers) are both friendly, high-energy people who can sacrifice their interests for the sake of others. When deciding between these points, ask yourself: Do I alter who I am to meet the needs of others (Caregiver), or am I fairly consistent about knowing who I am and what I need (Adventurer)?

Twos and Nines (Mediators) both merge with the agendas of others and have a hard time saying no. If deciding between these points, ask yourself:

Am I selective in terms of those with whom I merge (Caregiver), or does my attention seem to diffuse itself throughout the environment (Mediator)? Also: When entering a room of people I don't know, would I prefer to be noticed (Caregiver) or to blend in (Mediator)?

THREE (ACHIEVER) LOOK-ALIKES

Threes and Sevens (Adventurers) are both highly active, energetic individuals who tend to ignore the negative. If deciding between these points, ask yourself: If recognition comes my way, is it more because I earned it (Achiever), or because I'm entitled to it (Adventurer)?

Threes and Eights (Confronters) both exhibit leadership, determination and a strong penchant for action. If deciding between these types, ask yourself: When pursuing goals, is it important to be diplomatic and gain popular acclaim (Achiever), or just do what needs to be done and let feelings be damned (Confronter)?

SIX (LOYAL CYNIC) LOOK-ALIKES

Sixes (Loyal Cynics) who confront danger (counterphobic) and Eights (Confronters) are both confrontational, protective, and willing to fight for what they consider important. If deciding between these two types, ask yourself the following: When I am pushed, is my natural instinct to instantaneously recognize there will be consequences and then push back (Loyal Cynic), or to immediately push back and maybe consider the consequences later (Confronter)?

If you still need help in determining your type, please consult the Suggestions for Further Reading for suggestions of good print and online personality inventories.

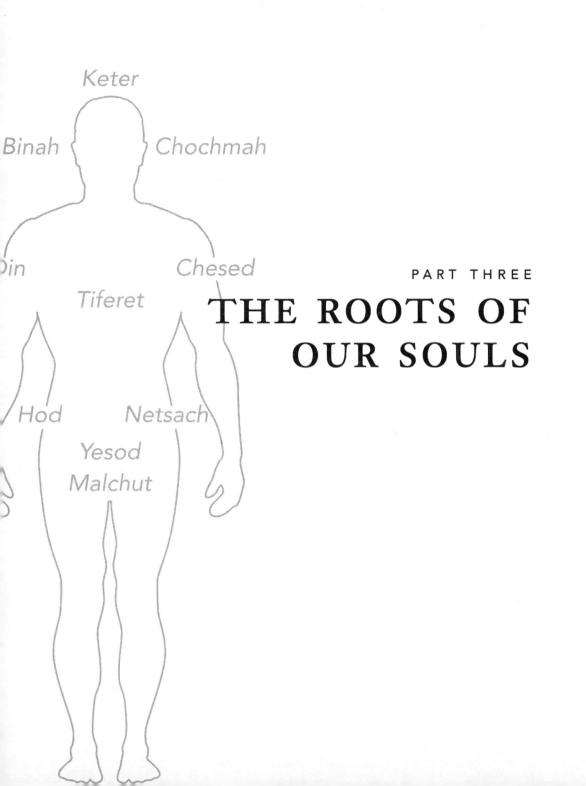

Keter

Binah   Chochmah

Din   Chesed

Tiferet

Hod   Netsach

Yesod
Malchut

PART THREE

THE ROOTS OF OUR SOULS

14

The Enneagram-Kabbalah Connection

Now that you have a preliminary idea of your personality type, let's examine the relationship between the Enneagram and Kabbalah. By comparing and contrasting the two systems, we may discover how they can help us grow and discover our lives' sacred tasks.

George Gurdjieff (1877–1949), an Armenian-born philosopher and spiritual teacher, is credited with introducing the Enneagram symbol to the modern West. The actual placement of the personality types around the diagram was accomplished by Oscar Ichazo (b. 1931), the founder of the Arica Institute in Arica, Chile.

Both Gurdjieff and Ichazo made reference to Kabbalah as having an effect on their work. In his book *Meetings with Remarkable Men*, Gurdjieff mentions a Jewish text entitled *Merkahvat*. Although there is no known text with that title, *merkahvah* (chariot) is the name of the first school of Jewish mysticism. Ichazo claimed that Metatron, who functions like a deputy God in Jewish angelology, revealed to him the placement of each personality type's emotional passion at its point on the Enneagram.[1] It is probable that kabbalistic influences on the modern Enneagram system can be traced back to the work of two medieval Christian Cabalists and spiritualists, Ramon Lull and Athanyus Kirscher.[2]

In addition, Kabbalah and the Enneagram were both influenced by many of the same sources. These include the Pythagorean and Neoplatonic schools of Greek philosophy, Gnosticism, Christian asceticism, and Sufism.³ Gurdjieff attributed the Enneagram symbol to an ancient wisdom school called the Sarmoun Brotherhood, which existed in the area of Mesopotamia near the end of the second millennium B.C.E. Kabbalah, which claims the biblical patriarch Abraham as its founder, asserts that Abraham's sons by his concubines went to live in that very place at the same time and became the "Wise Men of the East."⁴

When I first saw the Enneagram and learned of its different personality types, there seemed to be a ready correlation between it and Kabbalah's *Etz Chayim*, the Tree of Life.

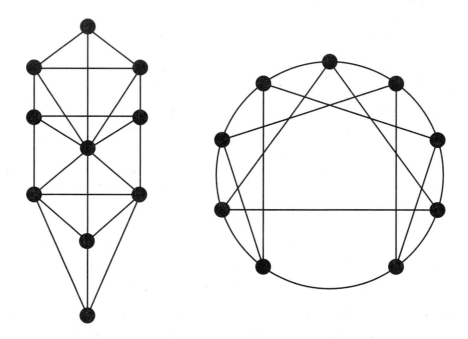

The twenty-two lightening-bolt pathways of the *Etz Chayim* convey the *Shefa*, or divine radiant energy, back and forth among the *sefirot*. The arrows, circle, and open six-pointed figure of the Enneagram represent the personality types, and the lines indicate that both are internally dynamic systems. Kabbalah maintains that we have three levels of soul, which correspond to the faculties of the Enneagram's three triads: *Nefesh*, the instinctual, *Ruach*, the emotional, and *Neshamah*, the intellectual. And both the Enneagram and Kabbalah claim that although our psyches potentially incorporate all the personality traits, each of us exhibits a predominant type or traces our soul's root back to a particular *sefirah*.

The following is a correlation of the *sefirot* and the Enneagram types:

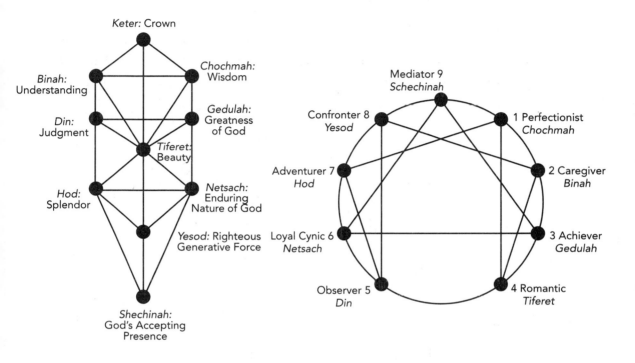

One: Perfectionist. *Chochmah*—the internalized Father, *Abba*, whose wisdom encompasses the potential perfection of all types.

Two: Caregiver. *Binah*—the Supernal Mother, *Ima*, whose understanding discerns and responds according to different needs and realities.

Three: Achiever. *Gedulah*—the expansive drive for greatness.

Four: Romantic. *Tiferet*—beauty and the yearning for completeness in a broken world.

Five: Observer. *Din*—the energy to enclose, to categorize, to set limits.

Six: Loyal Cynic. *Netsach*—steadfastness and the desire for surety.

Seven: Adventurer. *Hod*—seeking splendor within life.

Eight: Confronter. *Yesod*—the powerful, focused energy of the generative force, which can appear as *tsadik* (righteous) when seeking to redress perceived injustices.

Nine: Mediator. *Shechinah*—the accepting Presence, which takes in and mediates the perspectives and energy of the other *sefirot*.

One immediate question comes to mind: Where does *Keter*, the highest of the *sefirot*, fit into this schema? After all, there are ten *sefirot* but only nine Enneagram points. One answer: Only the soul of the Messiah emanates from *Keter*. As such, this highest *sefirah* cannot serve as the source for any of the specific human personality types we now find in the world.

A second answer lies in the fact that *Keter* serves as the point of transition from the essential, unbounded God—*Ayn Sof*—to the manifest characteristics of the nine lower *sefirot*. If we place those *sefirot* in a circular pattern, we have the following diagram:

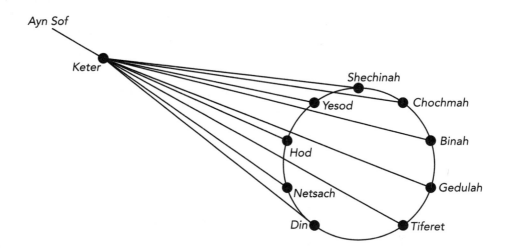

Thus we have *Keter* hovering over the other nine *sefirot,* funneling the *Shefa* from *Ayn Sof* to each. Conversely, as we seek to perfect our traits and actualize our own redemptive potential, we ascend back toward *Keter.* Thus, the most saintly representatives of all nine types begin to resemble one another more closely as they converge on the highest *sefirah,* the root of the messianic soul.[5]

15

A Study in Contrasts:
The Enneagram Outlook

As we've seen, there are many similarities between the Enneagram and Kabbalah. Both maintain that our personalities embody virtues and vices—which are not opposites but rather the flip sides of one another. However, the two systems differ significantly in their views of the human condition and our path to redemption.

According to Enneagram theory, each type has lost its connection to a specific aspect of Essence or the Divine, which is known as its *holy idea*. To compensate for this loss, each of us develops an *acquired personality*—a pattern of thoughts, feelings, and behavior derived from our experiences and innate temperament. This idea is based on a prevailing intellectual notion known as a *fixation* and a primary emotion known as a *passion*. These lead us to try to adjust for that which we feel is missing in our lives.

The following are short descriptions of how this dynamic works for each type:

ONE: PERFECTIONIST

By growing up in a world that judges and condemns, Perfectionists lose their connection to the holy idea of perfection: that all things and beings can be whole and right as they are. Perfectionists develop a fixation of resentment and a passion of anger as they seek to be worthwhile, by trying to perfect others and themselves.

TWO: CAREGIVER

By growing up in a world where they must praise others and cater to them to be rewarded, Caregivers lose their connection to the holy idea of freedom and will. They no longer know that they can be as they are and still receive what they need. They develop the fixation of flattery and the passion of pride, and believe that if they make themselves indispensable to others, their own needs will be met.

THREE: ACHIEVER

By growing up in a world where they are recognized only for what they accomplish, Achievers lose the holy idea of hope: that good can occur and that they can be cherished even if they don't make it happen. They develop the fixation of vanity in projecting a winning image and a passion for deceit in maintaining that image to gain the accolades of others.

FOUR: ROMANTIC

By growing up in a world in which they feel abandoned, Romantics lose their holy idea of idealism: that there is a deep, original connection among all things. They develop a fixation of melancholy, a sad yearning sweetened by hope, and the passion of envy, that others are gaining fulfillment they aren't, as they search for what is special and missing in life.

FIVE: OBSERVER

By growing up in an intrusive world that takes much and gives little, Observers lose the holy idea of omniscience: that they can know and grasp all that is. They develop a fixation of stinginess and a passion for avarice as they hoard their knowledge and ego resources, protecting their privacy against an imposing world.

SIX: LOYAL CYNIC

By growing up in a threatening world, Loyal Cynics lose the holy idea of faith in their own security and the good intentions of others. They develop the fixation of cowardice and the passion of doubt in remaining vigilant to protect their safety.

SEVEN: ADVENTURER

Growing up in a world of limitations that bring frustration and pain, Adventurers lose the holy idea of work: that their efforts can let them gain all they desire. They develop a fixation of constantly planning their next adventure and a passion of gluttony for every new pain-escaping and pleasure-increasing experience.

EIGHT: CONFRONTER

Growing up in an unjust world, Confronters lose their holy idea that there is a consistent truth, which applies equally to all. They develop a fixation of vengeance to right perceived wrongs, and a passion of lust to control situations and others so that they can shield their own vulnerability.

NINE: MEDIATOR

By growing up in a world that overlooked their views and made them feel unimportant, Mediators lose their holy idea of love: that they together with all others are equally cherished and valued. They develop a fixation of indolence and a passion for sloth, and are asleep to their own needs, as they seek to belong by subjecting and merging themselves into the agendas of others.

Our acquired personalities are not negative, for they help us navigate through life. There is nothing wrong, and much right, with wanting to be correct, to succeed, to be loyal, or to make peace. However, when these become the sole determining factors in our lives, we begin to feel as if we're trapped in a false self. Our patterns of behavior become so automatic and predictable that it seems as if we have no freedom to act otherwise. We are left wondering why we have to be so critical, why we feel that something is missing and we can't enjoy what we have, why we pick fights with others before they even insult us.

Different approaches have been prescribed to recover our holy idea and become the best versions of ourselves we can be. These include:

- Cultivating our virtue, which is the opposite of our passion. For example, Threes (Achievers) address their passion for deceit by being honest with others and brutally honest with themselves.
- Confronting and honestly dealing with our avoidance. For example, Eights (Confronters) should admit to being vulnerable in a situation rather than cover their feelings of weakness with bravado or flee from the situation.
- Embracing the higher qualities of our security point. For example, Fives (Observers) should adopt the assertiveness of Eights (Confronters).

The following chart details the virtue to cultivate, the avoidance to confront, and the security point qualities to embrace.

TYPE	VIRTUE TO CULTIVATE	AVOIDANCE TO CONFRONT	SECURITY POINT QUALITY TO EMBRACE
Perfectionist	Serenity	Anger	Spontaneity of Adventurer
Caregiver	Humility	Dependence	Recognition of own feelings of Romantic
Achiever	Honesty	Failure	Loyalty of Loyal Cynic
Romantic	Equanimity	Being ordinary	Objective standards of Perfectionist
Observer	Nonattachment	Inadequacy	Assertiveness of Confronter
Loyal Cynic	Faith	Helplessness	Acceptance of Mediator
Adventurer	Sobriety	Limitations	Introspection of Observer
Confronter	Innocence	Weakness	Caring of Caregiver
Mediator	Right action	Conflict	Productivity of Achiever

16

A Study in Contrasts:
The Kabbalah Perspective

The insights and prescriptions of the Enneagram provide us with powerful tools for self-understanding and growth. In his book *Tomer Devorah* (Deborah's Palm Tree), the eminent sixteenth-century Kabbalist Rabbi Moshe Cordevero offered spiritual practices for each *sefirah* that combine different aspects of the Enneagram approaches.[1]

If one looks carefully at the theory underlying the Enneagram, however, one could come away with a rather negative view of our human condition. Our connection to divine essence, our holy idea, has been lost. In response, we develop a false personality based on an emotional passion. That passion is derived from anger, deceit, or one of the seven deadly sins (fear, pride, envy, avarice, gluttony, lust, sloth) first detailed by the Desert Fathers, Christian ascetics who lived in Egypt during the fifth century.[2] It is little wonder that some find the Enneagram's perspective overly dark; if we've lost our link to the Divine and are mired in a false self based on a deadly sin, then we will have a hard time finding the joy and light in our personality types.

Kabbalah begins with the biblical premise that we are created in the "image of God." As such, divinity is not something we've lost but is something inalienably ours. That godly spark derived from the Tree of Life is who we really are. Therefore, we are:

NOT MERELY A	BUT ESSENTIALLY EMBODY
Perfectionist	*Chochmah*, the Wisdom of God
Caregiver	*Binah*, the Understanding of God
Achiever	*Gedulah*, the Greatness of God
Romantic	*Tiferet*, the Beauty of God
Observer	*Din*, the Judgment of God
Loyal Cynic	*Netsach*, the Steadfastness of God
Adventurer	*Hod*, the Splendor of God
Confronter	*Yesod*, the Righteous Generative Force of God
Mediator	*Shechinah*, the Accepting Presence of God

It is true that the roots of our souls can be cloaked by the *tselem*, that garment of our virtues and vices woven from our innate temperament, values, and experiences in this unredeemed world. The descriptions of the personality types in the previous chapters can help us identify and understand which *tselem* is ours. But we are not seeking to recover divinity lost; we are seeking to uncover the divine root of our soul, the place on the Tree of Life that is especially our own.

Perhaps more importantly, by recognizing the root of our own soul, we can begin to identify life's sacred tasks that God has uniquely reserved for us.

Rabbi Isaac Luria was a seminal Kabbalist, who lived in Safed in northern Israel during the sixteenth century. Although he died at the age of thirty-eight, his effect was far-reaching. To this day he is still commonly known as Ari, the Holy Lion.[3]

Like other Kabbalists, Luria believed that the early Genesis tales describe the outer manifestation of a sublime creative process unfolding within God—the creation of the divine personality embodied in the *sefirot*. However, for Luria, God's first formative act was not an outpouring of creative energy. Instead, it was an act of retreat.

Luria's basic premise is really quite simple. If *Ayn Sof*—the boundless, unknowable God—is everywhere, where is the room for everything else? To make space for the world, God withdrew into Godself, creating a vacuum with a divine residue left behind. Following this inward retreat, called *tzimtzum*, God sent forth beams of *Shefa*, divine radiant energy, into the void. These rays manifested the ten *sefirot* of the divine personality, whose most common configuration is the Tree of Life.

Following this event, however, an act of shattering importance occurred. The *Shefa* proved too powerful to contain, and burst the contours of the lower *sefirot*, much as the life force of a new plant's burgeoning tendrils cause it to burst its seed or bulb. This event, known as *Shevirat Hakelim*, the Breaking of the Vessels, rent the pathways connecting the *sefirot* and scattered *netsotsot*, sacred sparks, throughout existence. This cosmic shattering was later mirrored on the human level during the fall, when Adam's sin severed the tie that bound all human souls within his own.[4]

In our unredeemed world, we live in *Alma Deperuda*, a place of separateness and fragmentation. The Tree of Life is out of balance; we feel the limitations and judgments of *Din* more than we experience the expansiveness and grace of *Gedulah*. The presence of God's harmonizing and accepting nature, *Shechinah*, seems almost absent from our sense of the Divine. Just as our souls are covered by the *tselem* of our acquired personalities, the sacred sparks are obscured by shells of physical reality *(kelipot)*, much as the hard outer shell of a nut hides its edible, life-sustaining core.

Yet, amidst this brokenness, God has partners in the task of *tikkun*, repairing the fissures and restoring unity to the world. In response to *Shevirat Hakelim*, there are tasks of repair that all of us can and should perform, such as sheltering the homeless and feeding the hungry. As each of our souls is rooted in an individual aspect of God's personality as reflected through Primordial Adam *(Adam Kadmon)*, there are also *netsotsot*, sacred sparks, now hidden and spread throughout the world with a special affinity to each of our souls. Because we and they share the same divine origin and because of the unique confluence of our talents and life circumstances, each of us alone can liberate our particular sacred sparks and allow them to re-ascend to their rightful place on the *Etz Chayim*, the Tree of Life. It is only when all of the *netsotsot* have been released that cosmic harmony will be restored and universal redemption will be achieved.

No more telling example of the compelling uniqueness of our sacred tasks can be found than in the story of Bob. Bob, a teacher in the Midwest, married later in life. Despite fertility treatments, he and his wife were never fortunate enough to have biological children of their own. Some years ago, Bob's wife, Vivian, encouraged him to call his long-lost brother, Joe. Decades earlier, Joe had fled to the Southwest after a falling out with their parents.

Bob and Vivian soon went to visit Joe, who was in poor health. A widower, Joe was the sole caretaker of his sons, twelve-year-old Carl, and five-year-old Casey. From that point on, Bob and Joe stayed in touch. Bob helped Joe maneuver through various public assistance agencies. One weekend, Bob flew out to visit Joe and the children. On arrival, he discovered an ambulance in front of the apartment building. Joe had just died, leaving Carl and Casey orphans.

Reflecting back on the past several years, Bob said, "I just knew that God had called me to this particular situation. I told my wife that no matter what our religious observances or beliefs, we were being tested—and we had to step up."

"I knew that being their 'father' and yet not being their father would make the roles difficult for the boys and me. As a Romantic (type Four) I felt sure that I would have the emotional fortitude for this endeavor. Having the daily responsibility for these two young lives, however, has drawn me away from my penchant for self-absorption. Even though I'm now divorced, and the boys' only caregiver, I am sure that launching Carl and Casey successfully into manhood is one of my life's most important sacred tasks."

The chapters to follow will offer several different exercises that will train us to observe our behaviors and attitudes. They will help make us aware of our patterns in responding to life and of the sacred root of our souls, which lies beneath the patterns. By realizing the course of our life's journey, and who we essentially are, we might then be ready to start identifying which sparks are ours, and ours alone. We may hope that like Bob, but without tragedy, we will recognize which sacred tasks are ours uniquely to perform.

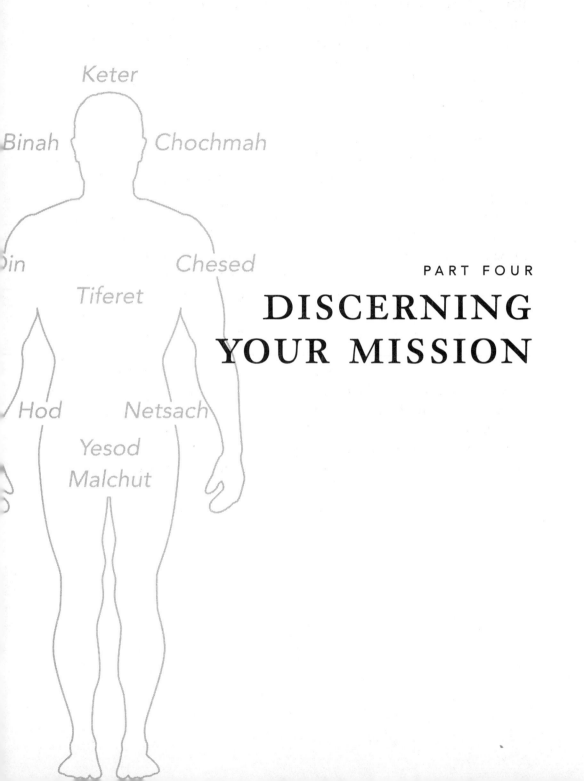

Keter

Binah · Chochmah

Din · Chesed

Tiferet

Hod · Netsach

Yesod

Malchut

PART FOUR

DISCERNING YOUR MISSION

17

Spacious Freedom Divine

In Jewish tradition, Psalms 113 through 118 are known as the Order of Praise, *Seder Hallel.* They speak of God's redemptive power and are recited at peak liturgical moments during the year, including Passover, Chanukah, and monthly at the New Moon.

The fifth verse of Psalm 118 makes an interesting assertion: "From narrow straits I called, 'Lord'; You answered me with spacious freedom divine." Most commentators believe that "narrow straits" refers to the cruel limitations of Egyptian bondage, whereas "spacious freedom divine" alludes to the Israelites' liberation during the Exodus through the leadership of Moses. Others see this as a model for understanding their own lives. When we feel constricted, as if all options are closed, God opens broad new vistas of opportunity for us.

One master, however, offered a unique insight into this verse.[1] "Narrow straits" refers to our own limited focus of attention, which restricts both our perspective on life and how we react to life's situations. We can be trapped by looking for flaws, causing us to automatically criticize. We can be trapped by looking for danger, so we automatically retreat. We can be trapped by looking for slights, so we automatically attack. "Spacious freedom divine" is the ability to pause between stimulus and response, to consider a wide range of options, and then to choose how we wish to respond. We can choose not to criticize a mistake, because preserving a friendship is more important.

We can choose to investigate whether a threat is real or imagined. We can ask what another's words really mean, rather than starting a fight.

It is this freedom to choose our responses which Viktor Frankl, founder of the Logotherapy school of psychology, considered to be the most vital human freedom of all. A Holocaust survivor, Frankl discovered that not even the degradation and inhumane conditions of Nazi concentration camps could take this freedom from those who were willing to claim it.[2]

HITBODEDUT AND OUR OBSERVING MIND

How do we develop the ability to pause and choose our responses? According to Jewish mystical psychology, each of us can isolate our consciousness from our imagination and our other perceptive faculties. This process is known in Hebrew as *hitbodedut*. While this word is used to connote meditation, it literally means "to isolate oneself." More than mere physical seclusion, it refers to the isolation of the most basic essence of the self, the "I" that lies behind our thoughts, memories, and fantasies.[3] In current meditation language, it is referred to as our "observer mind."

If you are not acquainted with your observer mind, let me propose a simple exercise—one I learned from my teacher, Helen Palmer. Find a comfortable, warm place where you will not be distracted.

1. Select a position, be it seated, lying down, or lotus, in which your head, heart, and abdomen are aligned, and in which you feel relaxed but alert.

2. Place your hands in your lap or on your thighs, or just let them hang loosely at your sides.

3. Close your eyes, or look softly ahead or downward without focusing on any particular object.

4. Take three deep breaths, each time exhaling twice the volume that you inhale.

5. Now, just allow your mind to think any thought that comes. Try to identify the content of the thought, who or what the thought is about.

6. Next, call to mind a memory: something that occurred in the past. Where were you? Who were you with? What did you experience, and how did you feel?

7. Let the memory go, and allow it to be replaced by a plan—something you'd like to do in the future. Where will you go? What will you do? Who, if anyone, will join you?

8. As the plan recedes, try to imagine that you are in Hawaii. Feel the sun warming your face, the sand between your toes. Envision the palm trees, the sea. Hear the rush of the waves. Rest in the beauty of that image. When you are ready to return, open your eyes.

This short practice should reveal to us something quite important. In a real sense we are not our thoughts, our memories, our plans, or our imagination. Behind all these wonderful mental and emotional processes is an "I," which can observe what we are thinking and feeling, which can pause and understand what is prompting our emotions and thoughts, which can choose how we will respond to the situations before us.

GOD'S PRAYER FOR YOU

Several easy exercises can open your awareness to the observing mind. You can close your eyes and over the course of a few minutes simply count the thoughts that occur to you. Don't try to analyze them or hold on to them. Just number them as a way of recognizing the "I" that lies behind your mental processes. If you prefer a more physically oriented practice, you might allot some quiet time and just count your breaths. Or slowly follow the course of your breath from your nostrils, down your trachea, all the way to the diaphragm, and then trace its course back up the body to the point at which you exhale. When you do this daily over a period of time, you can become even more familiar and comfortable with the function of your observing mind.

On a recent trip to Israel, I woke up and worshipped with a Sephardic (Middle Eastern rite) prayer group at the Western Wall. I prayed with a *siddur* (prayer book) that contained several kabbalistic devotional guides known as *kavanot*, and discovered fascinating notes appended to Psalm 145, known in Jewish tradition by its opening word, *Ashrei*. This psalm is arranged as an acrostic of gratitude to God. The Talmud promises that those who recite *Ashrei* three times daily—who chant God's praise from *aleph* to *tav* (A to Z) at sunrise, noon, and dusk—assure their place in the world to come.

This particular *siddur* added unique subscripts wherever the ineffable four-letter Hebrew name of God, YHWH, was written in the psalm. Under each of the ten appearances of YHWH was the name of a different *sefirah*. Looking closely, I found that each of the verses had a particular meaning for the personality type rooted in that *sefirah*. In a very real sense, these lines are our own divine prayer verses.

Here are the selections from Psalm 145, God's prayer for you:

Type One, *Chochmah*—for Perfectionists who are overly critical.
Gadol Adonai u-m'hulah m'od, v'li-g'dulato eyn chey-ker.
Great is the Lord and much praised; God's grandeur is beyond critique.

Type Two, *Binah*—for Caregivers who can be manipulative in their care for others.
Chanun v'rachum Adonai, erech apa-yim u-g'dol chased.
The Lord is gracious in compassion, patient, abundantly loyal, and kind.

Type Three, *Gedulah*—for Achievers who feel that reward comes solely through their unaided effort.
Tov Adonai la-kol, v'ra-chamav al kol ma-asav.
The Lord is good to all, and God's tender mercies embrace all God's works.

Type Four, *Tiferet*—for Romantics who feel melancholy and misunderstood.
Someych Adonai l'chol ha-nof-lim, v'zo-keyf l'chol ha-k'fufim.
The Lord is near to the fallen, and raises those bowed low.

Type Five, *Din*—for Observers who continually seek knowledge.
Yo-ducha Adonai kol ma-asecha, va-cha-sidecha y'var-chucha.
You shall be known, Lord, through all Your works, and Your faithful ones shall bless You.

Type Six, *Netsach*—for Loyal Cynics who find the world a fearful place.
Shomeyr Adonai et kol oha-vav, v'yet kol ha-r'shaim yash-mid.
The Lord guards those who love, but will strike down all the wicked.

Type Seven, *Hod*—for Adventurers who seek out and devour life's pleasures.
T'hilat Adonai y'daber pi, Vi-varech kol basar sheym kod-sho l'olam va-ed.

My mouth shall praise the Lord. Let all flesh bless God's holy name throughout the world forever.

Type Eight, *Yesod*—for Confronters who can impose on others.
Tzadik Adonai b'chol d'ra-chav, v'chasid b'chol ma-asav.
The Lord is just in all ways, but kind in all deeds.

Type Nine, *Shechinah*—for Mediators who are self-effacing.
Karov Adonai l'chol ko-rav, l'chol asher yik-ra-uhu ve-emet.
The Lord is near to all who call upon the Lord, to all who call upon the Lord in truth.

To become further aware of your observer mind through the message of your *sefirah*/type prayer verse:

1. Return to that comfortable place where you can pray undisturbed.

2. Select a posture that aligns your head, heart, and abdomen, representing the alignment of your thoughts, feelings, and instincts.

3. Imagine that you have placed yourself in God's tender, loving hands.

4. Breathe deeply three times, each time exhaling until you feel that you have no more air left inside.

5. In a relaxed but alert manner, slowly recite each word of your prayer verse, and repeat the verse again and again.

If you are new to this form of prayer, commonly known as mantra meditation, or in Hebrew as *Gerushin* or *Hagah*, begin with just five to ten minutes of repetition each day. Results do not always come immediately, so allow yourself at least a month for this practice. If after time your prayer remains dry, you might try to pray with a verse associated with your stress point or wing. These might better reflect what is currently going on in your life.

Although I am an Achiever, *Gedulah*, type Three, I began this practice with the passage "The Lord is near to all who call upon the Lord, to all who call upon the Lord in truth." This is the verse associated with my stress point, Mediator, type Nine, and it reflected some pressures I experienced at that time. Soon after I started, the verse began to reveal a world of new meanings to me. The Hebrew word for "near" is *karov*. It also connotes ritual sacrifice, engagement in battle, and a family relationship. I found myself asking God to accept my call as if it were an offering on the altar in Solomon's ancient temple in Jerusalem. I asked God to draw near to me and help me engage in the battle against my own rationalizations and deceits. I asked that I be worthy of being considered a relative of God.

Because honesty is the virtue of type Three, I began to see the word "truth" written vertically before me, from my head down to my abdomen. I felt reminded that if I were to be one of God's kin, my thoughts, my emotions, and my bodily instincts should all reflect personal integrity.

When my stress had abated, I felt comfortable switching to the verse for my own type: "The Lord is good to all, and God's tender mercies are over all God's works," and I began to notice God's goodness in all things. This helped me realize how naturally wonderful God's creation is, even without my efforts to produce any particular results.

During the next month, reflect on your ten minutes of daily meditation. Consider these questions:

- Which prayer did you select? (core type, wing, stress point, other.)
- What might your selection say about this moment in your life?
- Are you aware of any new insights about issues affecting you?
- Are the words taking on new meaning?
- How do you feel during the meditation and afterward?
- Do you feel moved to select another verse? Why?

That you might trace the course of your experiences with the exercises in this section, it would help to begin a Kabbalah diary. Following your meditation each day, please note your own observations in a diary. Are you aware of any new insights about core issues in your life? Did you observe any words taking on new meanings? Has your observer mind noticed that over time you react differently to your prayer?

You might choose to write in your journal for six days, and use the seventh day of the week to reflect on your week's diary and any pattern that may have developed. Feel free to pause on your tradition's day of rest, your Sabbath. Continue with this meditation practice and your journal for a full month.

18

Self-Observation and Self-Reflection

Now that you have become better acquainted with your observer mind, it is time to become better acquainted with yourself. For each of the next four weeks you are going to observe a different aspect of your behavior patterns, in an attempt to become aware of your deepest motivations. Record your responses to these exercises in your diary.

A twentieth-century Hasidic guide, Menahem Ekstein, offered a radical reinterpretation of a well-known verse from the Passover Eve table service, the *seder*. Traditionally, the sentence is read, "In each generation it is incumbent upon one to view oneself as if one personally has left Egypt." By splitting the sentence in two, we are offered this profound psychological insight: "In each generation it is incumbent upon one to observe oneself. This is as if one personally has left Egypt."

To begin this process of self-liberation, you will be asked to record and comment on your observed feelings and responses each day. Since Saturday is Shabbat, the Jewish day of rest and reflection, you might record your comments on Sunday through Friday and use Shabbat to review the patterns of your week's reactions and consider what that says about you. If your own tradition mandates a different day of rest, please feel free to use that day as your time for reflection.

WEEK ONE: PASSION

During the first week, observe daily instances when you responded emotionally with the passion of your type. What prompted your response? How did you feel as the event was unfolding—and afterward? How could you have responded differently? Continue with your observations and journal through the end of the week.

Type One, *Chochmah:* Perfectionist, Your Passion Is Anger

Why did you become angry? Did you feel that someone did something wrong or was getting away with something? Were you angry with yourself for committing a mistake or not living up to your own standards? How did your anger act itself out? Could you have reacted differently?

Type Two, *Binah:* Caregiver, Your Passion Is Pride

Were there times when you felt as if others couldn't get along without you? Did you use your offers of help to manipulate someone to do what you wanted? Did you find yourself recognizing another's needs while not knowing your own? Could you have reacted differently?

Type Three, *Gedulah:* Achiever, Your Passion Is Deceit

Were there occasions when you overstated your accomplishments or denied your defeats? Did you make your position or role sound more important than it really was? Did you rationalize your part in a failure or scapegoat someone else? Could you have reacted differently?

Type Four, *Tiferet:* Romantic, Your Passion Is Envy

Were there times you thought others were receiving something that you should have gotten? Did this make you feel unworthy or flawed? Did you feel sad or yearn for something you can't have or no longer can have? Could you have reacted differently?

Type Five, *Din:* Observer, Your Passion Is Avarice

Were there times when you thought the world was intruding on you? Did you refrain from meeting others or helping them because you would have felt depleted? Did you seek refuge in your own office, den, or room? Could you have reacted differently?

Type Six, *Netsach:* Loyal Cynic, Your Passion Is Fear

Were there times when you doubted the intentions of others without cause? Did you scan your surroundings for any lurking dangers? When something frightening occurred, did you flee, or confront it head on, to prove you weren't afraid? Could you have reacted differently?

Type Seven, *Hod:* Adventurer, Your Passion Is Gluttony

Were there times when you found yourself planning a whole number of exciting experiences all at the same time? Did you ignore some potentially hurtful consequence while searching for a good time? Did you cancel a previous commitment because something better came along? Could you have reacted differently?

Type Eight, *Yesod:* Confronter, Your Passion Is Lust

Were there times you found yourself wanting to eat, drink, party, or work to excess? Did you find yourself wanting to control those around you? Did you respond to others' gestures or looks as if they were intentional insults? Did you seek revenge? Could you have reacted differently?

Type Nine, *Shechinah:* Mediator, Your Passion Is Sloth

Were there times when you couldn't separate your own wants from those of others? Did you allow trivial secondary tasks to distract you from achieving important goals? Did you have a hard time saying no and instead just did not act? Could you have responded differently?

Mike's *sefirah* (personality type) is *Binah*, Caregiver. These are some of his observations:

- I gave advice to people knowing that they didn't want it. I could have asked questions and let them ask for advice if they wanted it.

- I felt myself to be unappreciated and attacked. I wondered what I did to deserve it. I could have become more of an observer, more quiet, or I could have just left.

- I felt more like an observer today, not involved in other people's problems, but just seeing them. I could have done exactly what I did— observe without intervening.

Now it's time for you to observe and record your own reactions. Once daily, for each of the next six days, note when you experienced the passion of your type, how you reacted, and how you might have responded more positively:

- I experienced _____ (your type's passion) when_____

- I reacted by _____

- I could have _____

Look back on your week's journaling during day seven, your Shabbat, and consider what it might reveal about yourself.

WEEK TWO: AVOIDANCE

There are situations that arise in our lives that we seek to avoid at all costs. Sometimes we might even feel it would be better to die than to face these situations.

During this week, try to observe how you react when those circumstances arise. What do you feel and what do you do? Ask yourself what costs you pay personally and in your relationships with others by this avoidance. Finally reflect on how you might grow as a person if you don't flee, but face the circumstance that you'd rather avoid. Try to notice one event each day, and record it in your diary throughout the week.

Type One, *Chochmah* (Wisdom):
Perfectionist, Your Avoidance Is Anger

Because anger is your passion, but "nice people" aren't supposed to rage, this emotion can be difficult for you. Did you quietly seethe when someone did something outrageous, took advantage of you, or criticized you unfairly? Was it hard to control your anger? Did you feel self-righteous afterward? What might have happened if you had relaxed your self-discipline, been "human," and appropriately vented your displeasure?

Type Two, *Binah* (Understanding):
Caregiver, Your Avoidance Is Dependence

How did you respond when you were in need and someone offered to help you? Was it difficult to receive rather than to give? Why? What might have occurred if you had depended on another to fulfill your needs, if you had been the gracious recipient?

Type Three, *Gedulah* (God's Greatness):
Achiever, Your Avoidance Is Failure

How did you react when a project or plan flopped? Did you shift the blame? Rationalize the circumstances? Present the results as a partial victory? Did you avoid an activity simply because you aren't good at it? What would happen if you actually risked looking silly, or admitted a defeat to others or to yourself?

Type Four, *Tiferet* (Beauty):
Romantic, Your Avoidance Is Being Ordinary

Did you pass up a purchase, a social occasion, or even a job because it seemed "run of the mill" or mundane? How did you feel when you were treated as just "one of the crowd" and not as someone special? What might happen if you stopped trying to always be viewed as unique?

Type Five, *Din* (Judgment):
Observer, Your Avoidance Is Inadequacy

How did you react when asked to answer a question or to give a presentation, and you didn't have all the facts? Did certain situations make you feel as if you were being robbed of your personal time and space? What were those situations, and how did you respond? What might happen if you weren't adequately prepared and you just went ahead anyway?

Type Six, *Netsach* (God's Enduring Nature):
Loyal Cynic, Your Avoidance Is Deviance and Helplessness

Did you see someone acting or expressing an opinion that went way outside acceptable mores? Were you asked to do or express something deviant? How did you feel, and what did you do? Did you find yourself in a threatening situation with no way to escape or respond? What was your first reaction? What might have happened in either instance if you had just "gone with the flow?"

Type Seven, *Hod* (Splendor):
Adventurer, Your Avoidance Is Pain and Limitation

What happened when an exciting new opportunity arose, and you discovered you already had plans for that time? How did you feel, and what did you do? What was your response to a friend's grief or to a situation that might have been hurtful to you? What might have occurred if you had kept your commitment, or confronted the hurt?

Type Eight, *Yesod* (Righteous Generative Force):
Confronter, Your Avoidance Is Weakness

Did a situation arise that made you feel small and incapable of meeting a challenge? What did you feel and how did you react? Did you experience a moment of emotional vulnerability—one that brought out the more tender feelings you usually try to hide? What might have happened if you had allowed yourself to actually be tender or weak?

Type Nine, *Shechinah* (God's Accepting Presence): Mediator, Your Avoidance Is Conflict

Did you find yourself in the middle of an argument? What were your feelings, and how did you respond? What happened when those who were arguing focused their disagreement on you? What would happen if you actually let others fight, or stood up for your own opinions?

Adam's *sefirah* is *Hod*, the Adventurer. Here are some of his reflections:

- I avoided my wife's depression by working all day and arranging to be out several evenings this week. I could have faced the situation by discussing the problem with her, letting her know how it's affecting me, and supporting her as she seeks help.

- I avoided my son's hurt during a difficult time of transition by keeping my plans to be out of town for a week, and then not only did I immediately return to work, but also I went out the first two nights that I was back. I could have faced the situation by altering my travel plans and forgoing my evening activities, so I could have been there for him through a tough time.

- I avoided discussing some contentious issues with a long-time friend. After pretending things were all right for a long time, I broke off the relationship. I could have faced the situation by stating my view in a way she could clearly understand, and working toward resolution.

It's your turn. Every day for the next week, record when you noticed your avoidance, how you responded, and how this encounter could help you grow.

- I avoided _____

- I could have faced the situation and _____

On day seven, spend time looking back over the week. What new insights did you discover about yourself?

WEEK THREE: STRESS

This week, please observe how you react to stressful situations. What specific conditions bring on your stress? Do you respond by exaggerating the more negative traits of your core personality type? Do you exhibit some of the less desirable characteristics of your stress point? Or does stress challenge you to respond in a more positive manner? If no stressful situation occurs during any given day, try to recall one from the past and how you reacted. Each day, journal the stress-producing situation and how you respond. If no stressful situation occurs, try to recall and record a stressful event from the past. Continue your journaling throughout the week.

Type One, *Chochmah:*
Perfectionist, Your Stress Point Is Four, the Romantic

Did you experience stress because life became chaotic, incorrect, or unfair? Did you find yourself becoming more critical than normal, consumed with putting things in order? Instead of seeing your actions as flawed, did you become depressed, wondering whether it is you who is flawed? Or, were you able to look beyond the rigid standards that usually govern your life and recognize what you really feel?

Type Two, *Binah:*
Caregiver, Your Stress Point Is Eight, the Confronter

Did you experience stress because you felt rejected by others or because your efforts went unappreciated? Did you become more cloying or try to make yourself indispensable? Were you aggressive and controlling, blaming and attacking others for perceived slights? Or, did you become more forth-right and less concerned about what others might think of you?

Type Three, *Gedulah:*
Achiever, Your Stress Point Is Nine, the Mediator

Did you experience stress because of failure, or feel unrecognized or over-whelmed by all you had taken on? Did you try to work even harder or seek additional recognition? Did you become listless and indifferent, losing yourself in TV or other distractions? Or, did you relax and become more accepting of things as they are rather than trying to make something happen?

Type Four, *Tiferet:*
Romantic, Your Stress Point Is Two, the Caregiver

Did you experience stress because you felt misunderstood or deprived of some fulfillment that should have been coming to you? Did you become depressed and unable to appreciate the blessings that you do have? Did you try to maneuver others to love you to fill some emptiness inside? Or, were you able to reach beyond yourself and help those around you?

Type Five, *Din:*
Observer, Your Stress Point Is Seven, the Adventurer

Did you experience stress because others were imposing on your time or space, or because you were not able to adequately master a subject? Did you withdraw further, or become more obsessive in your pursuit of knowledge? Did you begin to lose focus and take a "who cares?" attitude? Or, did you become less isolated and reflective by letting some of your inhibitions go?

Type Six, *Netsach:*
Loyal Cynic, Your Stress Point Is Three, the Achiever

Did you experience stress when you confronted a physically or emotionally threatening situation? Were you more guarded or more reckless in facing the threat? Did this challenge make you more task-oriented and concerned with how others perceive you? Or, did you become more resolute and effective?

Type Seven, *Hod:*
Adventurer, Your Stress Point Is One, the Perfectionist

Did you experience stress when you felt limited, as if life's pain and commitment were weighing you down? Did you respond by breaking promises and escaping to search for new pleasurable experiences? Did you become overly critical of others, blaming them because you were irritable or unable to have fun? Or, did you become more objective and careful in sorting out your alternatives for future action?

Type Eight, *Yesod:*
Confronter, Your Stress Point Is Five, the Observer

Did you experience stress when you felt weak or had your authority challenged? Did your behavior become excessive, controlling, or confrontational? Did you just want to be left alone, feeling isolated and besieged on all sides? Or, by stepping back, did you give greater consideration to the consequences of your actions?

Type Nine, *Shechinah:*
Mediator, Your Stress Point Is Six, the Loyal Cynic

Did you experience stress when faced with conflict or when others became overly demanding of you? Did you become less decisive and more stubborn? Did you find yourself becoming rigid, doubting yourself, and fearing whether anything would turn out right? Or, did you find yourself becoming more pragmatic and straight-thinking?

Linda's *sefirah* is also *Binah*, a Caregiver. The following are some of her observations:

- I experienced stress when I took my son shopping and resented him when he was ungrateful. I responded by becoming angry and confrontational. I grew by realizing that I could quietly explain to him how I felt and why he should be grateful.

- I experienced stress when I invited a friend to dinner for her birthday and she declined, because one of the other invited guests makes her feel uncomfortable. I responded by choosing not to make another date because of my anger. I grew through my realization that I could be more understanding.

You try now. Every day for the next week, record when you experienced stress, how you responded, and how this encounter could help you grow.

- I experienced stress when _____

- I responded by _____

- I grew through _____

Rest on day seven, and reflect on your entries for the past week. How might your cumulative discoveries aid in your growth?

WEEK FOUR: SECURITY

During this final week, please note how you respond when you feel safe and at ease. Does your behavior and mood change? Do you exhibit any of the positive traits of your security point? If you were to regularly cultivate these traits, might they lead towards your own personal growth? Or does the lack of pressure and challenge also bring out some less desirable characteristics in you?

You might begin the week by remembering a time when you felt completely loved and accepted. How did your personality change from the way you usually are? If you do not experience feelings of security on a given day during this week, try to reflect on a past occasion when you did, and record how you felt then. Each day, try to notice a moment of security. In your journal, note your observations about these times. If you do not experience a secure feeling on any given day, try to reflect on a past occasion, and record how you felt then.

Type One, *Chochmah:*
Perfectionist, Your Security Point Is Seven, the Adventurer

When feeling secure, were you more spontaneous and playful than usual? Did you become less judgmental and more accepting of others and yourself? When feeling carefree, did you also ignore the boundaries of proper behavior and become a bit excessive?

Type Two, *Binah:*
Caregiver, Your Security Point Is Four, the Romantic

When feeling secure, did you become more reflective and comfortable exploring your inner life? Were you able to recognize your own needs and express them to others without considering what they might think or what they might want from you? Did you also become more absorbed with yourself than normal?

125

Type Three, *Gedulah:*
Achiever, Your Security Point Is Six, the Loyal Cynic

When feeling secure, were you able to place loyalty to friends, coworkers, and family above your own advancement? Were you less concerned with your image and more at ease just being part of the group? Or did you also become a little more doubtful and indecisive?

Type Four, *Tiferet:*
Romantic, Your Security Point Is One, the Perfectionist

When feeling secure, were you able to judge things more objectively and less emotionally? Did you sense yourself acting more pragmatically and able to show greater self-control? Did you also become more critical of others and yourself?

Type Five, *Din:*
Observer, Your Security Point Is Eight, the Confronter

When feeling secure, did you become more assertive and forthright? Rather than retreating, did you act forcefully to defend yourself or advance a righteous cause? Did you become a little vengeful, ignoring the sensitivities of others?

Type Six, *Netsach:*
Loyal Cynic, Your Security Point Is Nine, the Mediator

When feeling secure, were you able to better see things from various perspectives? Did you feel less vigilant and more at ease, taking events as they came? Did you also feel a little distracted and indifferent to what was happening around you?

Type Seven, *Hod:*
Adventurer, Your Security Point Is Five, the Observer

When feeling secure, did you become calmer than usual, and more reflective? Were you willing to be more serious and examine matters extensively, seeing both the positive and the negative? Did you also withdraw into yourself to flee from commitment?

Type Eight, *Yesod:*
Confronter, Your Security Point Is Two, the Caregiver

When feeling secure, did you become more tender and lovable? Was it okay to reveal some of your own weaknesses while showing greater concern for the well-being of others? Or did you also become more cloying and make unreasonable demands of others?

Type Nine, *Shechinah:*
Mediator, Your Security Point Is Three, the Achiever

When feeling secure, did you become more focused and self-assured? Were you more energetic and comfortable in taking the lead? Did you also try to impress others by assuming more tasks than you could handle?

Patricia's *sefirah*, is *Chochmah*, the Perfectionist. These are some of her observations:

- I felt secure when I was outside bird watching. It's more than just a hobby to me. I responded with an ever-greater love and appreciation of nature. I felt almost transcendent when I let go of my critical mind and became absorbed with the soaring wonder of watching birds.

- I felt secure when I could drop my righteous demeanor and let my hair down. I responded by feeling at ease, and I was able to "party with the best of them." Traits that help me grow are the recognition by others that "you're not at all what we thought you were." I feel at times as if I have two different people in me, and this kind of affirmation helps me to further soften my rigidity and be more spontaneous.

Once again, it's your turn. Consider daily, for the next week, a time when you experience security and how you respond. Take special note of your feelings during these occasions.

- I experienced security when _____
- I reacted by _____
- I felt _____

On day seven, look back over your security experiences. Do you wish you could react more often as you did as they unfolded? Was this the "you"

you'd most like to be? Examine your journal for the past month, and then write down what you've learned that can help you attain this goal. Since most of us are impelled by our passions, and faced with avoidances, or are under stress far more often than we experience moments when we feel secure, jot down a few personal strategies that can help you be your best, most essential self.

Good work, and good luck.

19

How Did You Arrive?

We usually accept the notion that the past cannot be changed. "What's done is done," we are told, "so you might as well just move on." We might, however, pause to consider whether this truism is true.

The High Holy Day period is a focal point of the Jewish calendar year. The New Year, Rosh Hashanah, through Yom Kippur, the Day of Atonement, is a time of self-examination. According to one classical text, those who are unquestionably righteous are immediately inscribed for a year of blessing on Rosh Hashanah. Conversely, the indisputably wicked are condemned at that time. But what about those of us whose merits and shortcomings are equally balanced? We are told that if we repent during the interval between Rosh Hashanah and Yom Kippur, we too will be judged favorably.

This insight is very comforting, but it does raise a problem or two. First, if we are being judged on last year's deeds, that year ended at sunset on Rosh Hashanah Eve. How can the performance of divinely commanded, healing deeds in the New Year give us merit retroactively? And if *ex post facto* observance actually does figure in the accountings, why is it repentance alone and no other ritual or moral act that counts?

The answer: The reexamination of one's former life, and the shift in orientation that results from it, do change the past in a very real sense. The actual events cannot be undone. However, the value we place on them, and the deeds that will now emanate from them, can actually transform what had been defects, into the seeds for future growth. Conversely, acts of which we once boasted, may now seem like tears in the moral fabric of our lives that we feel compelled to mend.[1]

No better testimony was ever given to this transformational dynamic than that offered by the late chairman of the Republican party, Lee Atwater. Known for his smear tactics in the 1988 presidential campaign, including the Willie Horton commercial and his promise to "strip the bark off the little bastard," Michael Dukakis, Atwater was struck by inoperable brain cancer before his fortieth birthday. The following is his reexamination of his own past in an issue of *Life* magazine.

> I've come a long way since the day I told George Bush that his "kinder, gentler theme" was a nice thought, but I wasn't going to be. How wrong I was. There is nothing in life more important than human beings, and nothing sweeter than the human touch.
>
> I was one cocky guy. . . . My illness helped me to see what was missing in society was missing in me: a little heart and a lot of brotherhood. The 1980s were about acquiring—acquiring wealth, power, prestige. I know. I acquired more wealth, power, and prestige than most. But you can acquire all you want and still feel empty. What power I wouldn't trade for a little more time with my family![2]

Having now become aware not only of our own soul's root, but of the motivations that lie behind our actions, it might be clarifying to take a second look at the past. With greater insight into ourselves, perhaps we can now reevaluate the ups and downs of our lives, recognizing that perceived triumphs might have been sprinkled with a bit of self-aggrandizement, and that what we then considered failures might really have been no such thing.

One of the best ways to map and review the course of our lives is by constructing a timeline. By drawing a vertical or horizontal line, beginning with birth and ending with the current year, we can chronologically chart the moments of exaltation and despair, triumph and defeat. By placing those events we consider "high" points above or to the right of the line, and "low" points below or to the left of the line, we can try to discern recurring patterns and themes in our lives.

Here are two personal timelines with their attendant commentary. Meryl, who has moved from Long Island to Ohio, and then to Pennsylvania, is a

Confronter, type Eight, the *sefirah Yesod*. Who else but a Confronter would conceive of God as "the Big Guy upstairs"? Because Confronters are more disposed to action than to self-reflection, we should not be surprised that Meryl claims to have had few great revelations from this exercise. However, some interesting points emerge. Both her "to the right of the line" and "to the left of the line" moments are bound to issues of protecting her children and family loyalty—issues of special importance for an Eight. Even though she placed her relocation to Ohio below the line, she identified with a divine calling to crusade against the perceived injustice of the Christmas activities at her Columbus public school, which she viewed as a breach of the wall between church and state. While aching for herself and her daughters over the loss of her mother and her husband Larry's mom, she again was able to recognize a redemptive future in those losses. Ours is a society that socializes against women's being assertive, often labeling them as unfeminine, aggressive, and heartless. By honoring her late mother and standing on her own, Meryl has grown comfortable in her own Confronter/*Yesod* skin.

In her timeline notes, Meryl relates:

> My "to the right of the line" (high) moments were all times representing positive events in my life cycle. All were times of growth, either personal or familial. They all came from very natural or gut reactions. I am able to focus on others when I am secure.
>
> My "to the left of the line" (low) moments were times of loss or injury. I definitely revert to the *Din* (Observer, Five, stress point) personality during these times. When I am low, I do not like or want to share my pain with others I do not trust or know well.
>
> Few new lessons occurred to me regarding my reactions to important events.
>
> Almost all were family oriented. It is when people close to me leave or, like my parents and Larry's, die that I feel most hurt. My dad's surgeries and Larry's were scary because of their unknown results—results I could not control.
>
> God has been with me through my life. I have sought God's help in good times and bad. Even before this exercise, I thought of God as the "Big Guy upstairs."

131

	1957	Birth
	1960	Brother's Bar Mitzvah
	1961	Preschool
	1968	Graduated elementary school
	1969	Bat Mitzvah
Mother got ill; grandfather died	1970	
	1971	Graduated Jr. high school
Mother's surgery and chemo	1972	
	1974	Graduated high school
	1976	Brother married
Had tonsils out	1978	Graduated college
	1979	Married
	1980	Bought first house
	1981	Summer, went across country
	1982	Heather born
Grandma died	1983	
Moved to Cleveland; mother-in-law died	1984	
	1985	Jenni born
Moved to Columbus; mother died; sister-in-law's baby died	1987	
	1988	Carly born
	1989	First niece adopted
Knee surgery; family problems	1994	
	1995	Heather's Bat Mitzvah
	1997	Found out moving to PA
	1998	Jenni's Bat Mitzvah
Father's failing health; feeling helpless	1999	

I am not really sure where my life has led to this point! I strongly feel things happen for a reason. I feel we moved to Columbus so that I could advocate for the Jewish elementary children not being subjected to Christian religious education in the public schools in December.

Certainly, moving away from Long Island and my family softened the realization of the losses of my mother and Larry's mother on the everyday lives of our family. If our children had been around the rest of the family more, our mothers' deaths would have been in the forefront of their minds. (They are in mine.)

I also feel cheated that my children did not have the love of their grandmothers—a love that cannot be replaced.

Being away from my family, I do feel I was able to step up from the way "girls are supposed to act," to be like my mother was. She fought for what she believed in. But I was in her shadow . . . intimidated. The more I am getting to know myself, the better I like myself!

Mike, whom we met earlier, is a self-confessed type Two, a Caregiver/*Binah*. It is interesting to note how his positive experiences have led him to value emotional depth, the higher side of his security point, Four, the Romantic. He speaks of his low periods as springboards to growth. When he learned it was okay to just be alone with God, he learned that he didn't have to draw his worth solely from relationships and obsessively catering to others.

In his timeline notes, Mike relates:

> The moments that I value so highly to the right of the line were deep emotional times. They were moments of great learning for me. I was able to learn more deeply what love was really about. I learned love, trust, and, probably more than anything else, hope.
>
> I considered the times to the left of the line to be very hurtful, but now I realize that they were the moments of greatest growth. Through the pain, I realized more fully that God did exist. It was as if there was nothing else, so there had to be God.
>
> Being a type Two (Caregiver), I had feelings of guilt when my mother died, and abandonment when my wife left me. I felt I couldn't give enough, but I never gave to myself. I was always last or not at all.

133

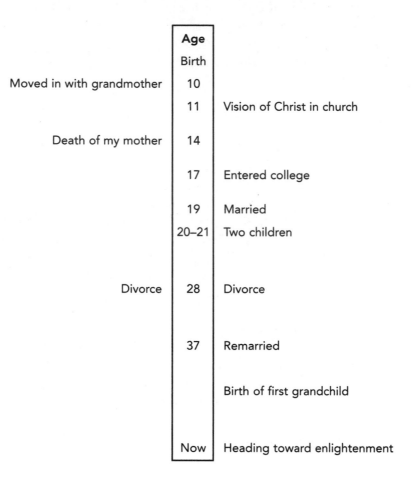

	Age	
	Birth	
Moved in with grandmother	10	
	11	Vision of Christ in church
Death of my mother	14	
	17	Entered college
	19	Married
	20–21	Two children
Divorce	28	Divorce
	37	Remarried
		Birth of first grandchild
	Now	Heading toward enlightenment

I thank God for all the experiences I've had in my life. The people and events were springboards for me to know myself better and to grow more spiritually. New lessons are always arising both in the extremes and in everyday life.

I don't see any pattern in the ups and downs, except that the learning experiences were equal. God has been involved in all the events in my life. I believe I am being led to a place of self-actualization.

> For me, being a Caregiver is like looking in the past, or at old pictures. It also makes me look at other people of the same type, and I see where I've been.

As a prelude to discovering your tasks for the next chapter of your life, take a look back at where you've been. Draw a line, labeling its left end point Birth and its right end point Now:

Birth _____ Now

In chronological order, place the occurrences that you consider high points in your life above the line. Similarly, place the lows below the line.

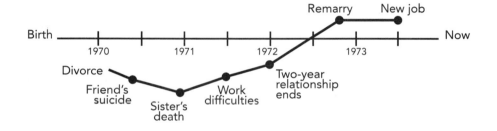

The example above charts, in part, the life of Alana, an Achiever. It shows a severe two-year trough, followed by a significant crest. When she looked back at this period on her timeline, she began to appreciate how the losses of 1970–1972 helped to teach her the preciousness of relationships and put her in touch with her deep, inner feelings—issues she as an Achiever had previously suppressed. When she viewed her timeline in retrospect, she began to recognize how her subsequent remarriage and job change, both uplifting events, were motivated by her Achiever's desire to avoid the stigma of failure associated with divorce and work difficulties. Seeing this alternating pattern of sustained troughs and high crests throughout her timeline, Alana realized that her extended lows, rather than being times of pure sorrow, were necessary periods of cleansing and preparation for her next period of ascent that seemed to follow.

Now plot your own timeline, and consider your life to this point. Like Meryl, Mike, and Alana, what subtexts have your *sefirah*/type provided in the unfolding drama of your life? Are your highs and lows just random, or do they reveal an unfolding pattern or trajectory in your life? Where are you at this point, as you anticipate what is yet to come?

20

Corresponding with God

The following exercise will take sixty to ninety minutes. You will need a quiet space, which should be darkened, and yet light enough to allow you to write. In addition, you will need these objects: table, chair, candle and holder, pen, and plenty of paper.

Before beginning the practice, please read through this entire chapter. Then, when you feel centered and the time is free of interruption, try the exercise in its entirety. Don't worry if during the exercise you don't see visions unfolding in your mind, but only experience a sense of something transpiring. As I like to say, there's no such thing as flunking Jewish meditation.

BURNING THE LEAVEN

On Passover, Jews are bidden to eat *matzah*, unleavened bread. Unlike the flat *matzah*, which appears humble and is all natural, leavened baked goods are associated with that which is self-inflated and artificial. In preparation for the *Pesach*, the Feast of Liberation and Renewal, we take candles and search every corner of our homes for remaining crumbs of leaven, which we then burn the next morning.

To ready ourselves for the renewal that comes from learning which sparks are uniquely ours to liberate, we too must purge the "leaven" from our being. As we said earlier, some Kabbalists have envisioned the *sefirot* in the human form of *Adam Kadmon*, Primordial Adam. Thus, each of the *sefirot*/points has its own location on the body.

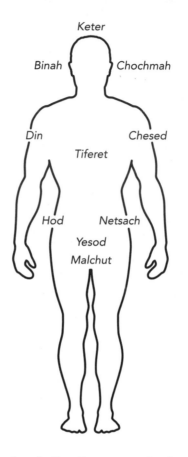

To strip away the *kelipot*, the shells of your acquired personalities' passions and fixations, so that the divine essence of your type can shine through:

1. Place a lighted candle safely on the table.

2. Darken the room, and sit facing the candle in a relaxed, yet alert and comfortable posture with your head, heart, and abdomen aligned, and both feet on the floor.

3. Take three deep breaths, exhaling twice as slowly as you inhaled.

4. Focus softly on the candle as all other objects recede from view. Kabbalistic meditators teach that in addition to seeing the white, yellow, and

red shades of the flame, the adept can also see the black aura surrounding the flame, upon which God initially wrote the Ten Commandments, and the blue fire of the electrum seen by Ezekiel in his vision of God's Chariot Throne.[1]

5. As you concentrate on the flame, you might wish to repeat quietly: *Kee nair mitzvah v'Torah ohr* (God's command, a lamp; God's guidance, light).

6. When you are ready, close your eyes and imagine the light beaming slowly, and in sequence from the candle to:

a. Your right eye, purging resentment and anger, so you can serenely behold the perfection of God's Wisdom as embodied in creation (*Chochmah*, type One).

b. Your left ear, banishing flattery and pride, so that you uncover the humility and will, to listen with the Understanding of God (*Binah*, type Two).

c. Your right arm, searing away deceit and image, so that in hope and honesty you can reach for the Greatness of God (*Gedulah*, type Three).

d. Your heart, eliminating envy and melancholy, so that you might gain balance as you open to the Origin and Beauty of God (*Tiferet*, type Four).

e. Your left arm chasing stinginess and greed, so that you can release attachments, and know the discerning Judgment of God (*Din*, type Five).

f. Your right leg, dissolving cowardice and fear, so you might walk courageously with faith in God's Enduring Nature (*Netsach*, type Six).

g. Your left leg, shining through your escapist plans and appetites, to reveal the sobriety and true work that are the Splendor of God (*Hod*, type Seven).

h. The place on your body where you associate male generativity, burning away lust and vengeance, to uncover the truth and innocence that are the Foundational Righteousness of God (*Yesod*, type Eight).

i. The place on your body where you associate female generativity, removing indolence and being asleep to yourself, so that love and right action unveil the Accepting Presence of God (*Shechinah*, type Nine).

7. Even if you don't recall the specific vices, virtues, and divine characteristics of each type, just let the candle's glow illuminate the sacred in each aspect of your body.

8. When you are ready, imagine the light glowing from each of the nine locations within you. Allow these nine beams of light to emanate from you, until they all merge with the single flame of the One.

9. Bask in the radiance pulsating back and forth between the candle and you. When you are ready to return, open your eyes.

LETTERS

Now quietly turn on the lights, and write two letters. The first is from you to God, addressing these issues:

1. The three sacred tasks you feel are uniquely yours to perform during the next chapter of your life.

2. Why you think you are particularly suited to perform them.

3. What you will be willing to change, and even give up in your life, to accomplish these tasks.

Once you finish, write a letter back to yourself from God. Have God speak to these matters:

1. What God thinks of your tasks.

2. What different tasks God might have for you.

3. What God will ask of you and grant to you, as you seek to elevate these sparks.

As you write these letters, don't censor your thoughts. Keep your hand constantly moving with the pen, and write down everything that occurs to you. Whether you believe that your ideas are flowing directly from God, solely from your subconscious, or from God through your subconscious, what you write might really shock you.

    Here are some actual letters representing the insights by some who have engaged in this divine correspondence. This set of letters is written by Ilene, a type Six (*Netsach*, Loyal Cynic):

Dear God,

I would like to connect with my higher being so that I can radiate out a positive energy—a loving energy to those around me—family, friends, anyone I come in contact with. I would like to be an uplifter. I also would like to continue to create new things—new paintings that heal and uplift others and myself—and to be more motivated and energetic in this direction. New ways of giving confidence to my students and my family.

I would like to communicate clearly with those who have made their transitions until the end of my physical life. This would help in my evolving and, hopefully, in theirs too. I would like this communication to be visual, auditory, every sense possible to receive and then radiate out again to others. Please help me, God, be all that I came to be. I love you.

Letter from God

Spread your love and uplift others—to raise the vibrations of those around you. Create all kinds of experiences with me, experience and add to my creation. Communicate and send love, receive messages and love from those who have departed. Hopefully, one day there will be no void of separation—all will be one, peacefully, lovingly.

Let this thought resonate within you and feel good. Accomplish these things and create new reasons for being alive; be an uplifter to yourself and others.

I send my love and encourage you to renew strength from your goals, and I will add more, as each day continues.

Your dad is with you; he guides you and is always sending his love to you and to those who love you.

The author then closes with "Thank you, God."

The next letter from Stan, a type One (*Chochmah*, Perfectionist), represents an inner dialogue with God rather than two separate letters:

Dear God,
Three things:
    1. Have my children become independent.

My children are my responsibility.

2. Do something good that will last after me.

I am unique, and I have unique abilities that could be used to benefit many, perhaps all.

3. Redirect my life from vanity, idleness, pride, anger, diffusion, doubt, fear, pain, withdrawal, aggression, frivolity toward greater knowledge, good, reduced pain, divinity, wisdom, wholeness, separateness, and courage.

My life is mine and my responsibility.

I don't know how to do this. I know, but I don't know. I fear failure. Failure is only a step, perhaps a beginning. I have seen light and felt warmth. I can give some of that ability to others through you.

I fear loving, knowing there should be no fear. Others love me. Maxine smiled when I first saw her; Maxine makes me smile. I can't love all, but I can show more. Would others want that? Does that matter? I must follow my path of rightness regardless of what others may want.

It matters little or not at all whether anyone else would appreciate that; some may, some will, some will not.

I should do more to help, be calmer, smile, sing, truly laugh rather than just jest. Open my eyes, see and learn. Whatever I know, there is more to learn, use, and do.

It is okay if what I accomplish is small, as long as it is done. Why is it done . . . to be perfect? No, to help perfect the world, even if just a small part.

I don't find this easy. I should calm my heart more; my feelings can lead me. Should I let them? I can, I should, I will. What I need and am is both inside and outside of me. I can find both and help perfect myself. Then I can help perfect the world and be an example to others. I don't need others to do this for me; I need to do it for myself. It is all within me and just outside of me. It is. It always has been. It always will be.

I need to know this for what it is and what it is not, for what it could be, because I am part of the world.

A still, small voice—more than a whisper. Why am I doing this? Does it matter? Yes, it should.

This last set of letters is written by Marge, an interfaith minister, who performs wedding and nontraditional commitment ceremonies. Still unable to decide whether she is a Two (*Binah*, Caregiver) or an Eight (*Yesod*, Confronter), she relates that her friends are pretty sure she is an Eight.

Dear God,

You have set me on an amazing path. I'm not sure I know of three things, but I hope so. Aha, maybe they're starting to come to me.

First, God, I want to deepen my relationship with you. I want to know you better; there is so much to learn. Who are you? Where do I fit into all of this? My life's journey has been a journey toward you—of this I am sure. Show me how. I am so oriented to doing the things of life and finding you there, or so I think. Show me new ways to you. I know you want this of me.

Second, I want to live with Tom in the deepest love relationship possible. I want our love affair to continue, growing deeper, not diminish with the passage of time. I want our sexual relationship to continue to bring us pleasure, comfort, and joy. I want our sexual love to reflect our love for each other, and I want it to celebrate our love for you. I want this great love affair to radiate out from us and touch our children and theirs, our families and friends. I so want for Tom and me to be the lovers of lovers!

Three, I want my ministry to become the gift to humanity that I think you have helped me create it to be. I feel sure that it is one of the places where the divine sparks fell, took root, and are blossoming.

Help me know what to do to nurture this growth. Help me find people and resources that I will need. God, this ministry is the most amazing gift. Show me how to use it to perfect your reign on earth. Your kingdom come! Give me the wisdom and insight to make this happen. The Rabbi said that God created all, then stepped back in restraint to allow creation to happen. This is the self-creating universe of creation spirituality. Show me how to do this with this divine creation of mine.

I have always loved you, God. Blessed is your name. Your faithful daughter.

Letter from God:

My darling daughter,

How I love it when you write to me. I don't even mind that it is an assignment! Thank you for bringing so much of yourself to everything you do. I see you bring yourself down in the details sometimes. You have this terrible feeling that you won't get everything done that you feel called to do. But you know what? What you finish is what I want you to finish. Please meditate on that, and put it out of your mind.

Of course I want you to draw closer to me—in your own consciousness of our closeness. You know you walk in the light—you say so all the time! I would like you to enjoy me more. You're beginning to do that with the Enneagram, even though what you learn sometimes brings pain. But lately you are so connected, I know you're having fun.

Your relationship with Tom is a joy to the universe! Your love and marriage is a divine dance that I love to watch. Try to keep the problem of the kids in its proper place, and use your relationship for the life of the world. Do you realize how deeply your ministry is connected to your marriage? Your marriage gave birth to it and nourishes it. Draw upon the gift of your marriage as you open up your ministry. You will learn what this means. Meditate on your love and marriage and use it to expand your consciousness of your ministry. (God? What does this mean?) Just do it. Your answers will be revealed. You will know where to go when it is time.

I do want your ministry to spread and grow and give life to the world.

You are indeed my precious daughter. You have given so much of your life to me and for me. I will lead you. You will know.

Your faithful One.

Prepare your room, your chair, your candle, your table, and your journal. Ready yourself to receive the purging and illuminating light of God, and then enter into divine correspondence about your life's next sacred tasks . . .

Final Thoughts:
The Willingness to Try

The following story is told of Rabbi Yaakov Yitzhak Rabinowitz, the Holy Jew of Pshyshka.

> One day the Holy Jew was walking along the road outside his village. He came across a Polish farmer, whose wagon had overturned.
>
> "Help me right my wagon," called the farmer.
>
> "I can't," said the Jew. "It's much too heavy for me."
>
> "No, it's not," retorted the farmer. "It's not that you can't. You just don't want to try."
>
> The Jew and the farmer put their backs into it—and, lo and behold, they righted the wagon.
>
> Returning to the town, the *rebbe* recounted the story to his students.
>
> "I learned something important from that encounter," said the Jew.
>
> "What's that, *rebbe*?"
>
> "That even if the Divine Presence is now in exile, we can still uplift those languishing sparks waiting for us. The issue is not 'Can we?' 'It is Are we willing to try?'"[1]

So too with us. Having some sense of the divine root of our souls and the sacred tasks that lie before us, the question is not "Can we achieve this?" Surely we can. The challenge before us now is to summon our will to try.

NOTES

CHAPTER 1

1. Martin Buber, *Tales of the Hasidim, Later Masters* (New York: Schocken Press, 1972), 252.

CHAPTER 2

1. Babylonian Talmud, Mishnah, *Sanhedrin* 4:5.

2. Genesis 2:7. The Hebrew verb used to describe Adam's creation is the same term used for character inclination *(Yetser)*. The doubling of that term's first letter *(va-Y Yetser)* led Jewish sages to claim that each person has two character inclinations.

3. For a more detailed comparative study of these systems, see my *The Enneagram and Kabbalah: Reading Your Soul* (Woodstock, Vt.: Jewish Lights, 1998).

CHAPTER 3

1. Among the most important differentiations of people of the same type, but beyond the scope of this introductory study, are the instinctual subtypes. One's personality type can take on a specific slant depending on whether one is normally most concerned about ensuring personal welfare (self-preservation), issues of status within groups (social), or intimate relationships (sexual or one-on-one). For further information, see Helen Palmer's *The Enneagram* (San Francisco: HarperSanFrancisco, 1991) or *The Enneagram and Kabbalah*.

CHAPTER 14

1. On *merkahvah:* G. I. Gurdjieff, *Meetings with Remarkable Men* (New York: Dutton, 1969), 90. On Metatron: Helen Palmer, *Vice to Virtue Conversion,* (Loyola University, International Enneagram Association Conference, 1996, Creedance Tapes).

2. See James Webb, *The Harmonious Circle* (New York: G. P. Putnam & Sons, 1980).

3. See Moshe Idel, *Kabbalah: New Perspectives* (New Haven: Yale University Press, 1988), 9, 13, and 15; and Gershom Scholem, *Kabbalah* (New York: Times Books, 1974), 25, 27, 35, 37, and 49.

4. Genesis 25:6

5. Modern Enneagram theorists refer to this as convergence. The most highly evolved of each of the types bear, perhaps, even greater resemblance to one another than to average representatives of their own types. Conversely, as the different types degenerate into pathology, they begin to more closely resemble each other.

CHAPTER 16

1. See The *Enneagram and Kabbalah*, Sections I and II.

2. Evagrius of Pontus, *The Praktikos*, is the first listing. Evagrius actually included an eighth passion, Vainglory, which corresponds to the image-consciousness of the Achiever.

3. The acronym *Ari* stands for Elohit Rebbi Itzhak, the divine Rabbi Isaac.

4. Gershom Scholem, *The Messianic Idea in Judaism* (New York: Schocken, 1971), 456.

CHAPTER 17

1. See Nosson Scherman, *The Haggadah Treasury* (New York: Mesorah Publications, 1980), 151.

2. Viktor Frankl, *Man's Search for Meaning* (New York: Simon & Schuster, 1984).

3. Aryeh Kaplan, *Jewish Meditation* (New York: Schocken Books, 1985), 52.

CHAPTER 19

1. Solomon Morganstern, in *Chains of Gold*, Vol. IV (Skokie, Ill.: Hebrew Theological College Press, 1992), 1–2.

2. In Jack Reimer, *The World of the High Holy Days* (Miami, Fla.: Bernie Books), 19–20.

CHAPTER 20

1. Kaplan, *op. cit.*, 69.

FINAL THOUGHTS

1. Buber, *op. cit.*, 228.

GLOSSARY

Acquired Personality: Our habitual pattern of thoughts, feelings, and responses to life's situations, derived from our experience and our innate temperament. We need the acquired personality to negotiate through life, but it can smother our real, essential self.

Arrows: The directional lines that connect the Enneagram personality type points to one another. Movement with the arrow, such as 1 → 4, is toward one's stress point. Movement against the arrow, such as 8 ← 2, is toward one's security point.

Enneagram: A nine-pointed starlike diagram used to chart the unfolding of the human psyche.

Essence: The original, undivided unity of all being.

Essential Self: The aspect of self that is manifested when we feel at one with the world, experiencing no conflicts between our thoughts, instincts, and emotions.

Fixation: The mental image we form to compensate for the particular aspect of essence we feel we have lost.

Holy Idea: The aspect of essence we feel we have lost while responding to the tensions and experiences of life.

Instinctual Subtype: A means of differentiating personalities within the same type based on our three instincts for survival. Those most concerned with personal well-being are self-preservation subtypes. Those most concerned with intimate relationships, the propagation of the species, are sexual subtypes. Those most concerned with issues of group status, one's place in the herd, are social subtypes.

Passion: Our chief emotional trait developed to compensate for the aspect of essence we feel we have lost.

Point: The nine individual numbers on the Enneagram, each representing a different basic personality type. In Enneagram literature, these points are also referred to as type or style.

Security Point: The personality type whose higher traits we emulate when we are feeling comfortable and secure. These are indicated by movement against the arrow within the Enneagram, so that 3 ← 6 indicates that Six is the security point of Three.

Stress Point: The personality type whose lower traits we exhibit when we experience distress. These are indicated by movement with the arrow, so that 2 → 8 indicates that Eight is the stress point of Two.

Triads: The division of the nine Enneagram types into three groups of three based on their predominant personality faculties. Points Eight, Nine, and One are the instinctual or "Belly-Centered" triad because persons of these types react to experience primarily through bodily instinct. Points Five, Six, and Seven are the "head-centered" triad because these persons respond primarily through thinking. Points Two, Three, and Four are the "heart-centered" triad because these persons respond primarily through emotion.

KABBALAH

Adam Kadmon: The humanlike configuration of the ten traits of God's personality as Primordial Man, based on the idea that humans are shaped in the divine image.

Ayn Sof: The boundless, seamless, unknowable God.

Binah: Understanding. The ability to discern different realities and needs and to respond accordingly. Since "being" differentiates within *Binah* into the ideal forms of objects and creatures the way a zygote develops into a fetus of organs and limbs within the womb, *Binah* is also called *Ima*, Supernal Mother.

Chochmah: Wisdom. The encapsulation of all perfect possibilities before those possibilities unfold. Since *Chochmah's* pristine content is encoded much the way DNA is encoded within seed, this *sefirah* is also referred to as *Abba*, Supernal Father.

Din: Judgment. The aspect of God that sets limits and boundaries. *Din* is to *Chesed* as form is to content. Also called *Gevurah*, the manifestation of divine power.

Etz Chayim: The configuration of the ten traits of God's personality as the Tree of Life.

Gedulah: Greatness. The creative force of God's love, also known as *Chesed*, the higher expressions of loyalty, kindness, and piety.

Hitbodedut: "To isolate oneself," in Hebrew.

Hod: Splendor. Divine majesty or splendor. *Hod* refracts and conveys the defining energy of *Din* to the lower world, thus keeping the forces of chaos and entropy at bay.

Karov: Near, in Hebrew. It also connotes ritual sacrifice, engagement in battle, and a family relationship.

Kavanot: Kabbalistic devotional guides.

Keter: Supernal Crown. The transition from potential to actuality, from the unknowable *Ayn Sof* to God's revealed personality.

Metatron: A deputy God in Jewish angelology, who is claimed to have revealed the placement of each personality type's emotional passion at its point on the Enneagram.

Merkavah: Chariot, in Hebrew. Also the name of the first school of Jewish mysticism.

Netsach: Endurance. The enduring, steadfast nature of God. *Netsach* filters the divine grace of *Gedulah* and helps channel that expansive, creative energy to the lower world.

Netsotsot: Sparks of divine light, which were scattered throughout the world during *Shevirat Hakelim*. By performing God's commandments, *mitzvot*, with the proper intention, we can lift these sparks back to their source in the *Etz Chayim* and hasten world redemption.

Ratso Va-Shov: "Egress and Return," the continual movement of the divine radiance along the twenty-two pathways that connect the *sefirot* along the *Etz Chayim*.

Sefirot: The ten manifestations of the divine personality. For a detailed list and description of the *sefirot*, see chapter 2.

Shechinah: Accepting Presence. God's accepting presence, which receives the *Shefa*, divine energy, from *Tiferet* and *Yesod* and mediates its blessings to our world. Like *Binah*, it is a feminine aspect of God and is described as a sister or bride. The closest *sefirah* to our world, *Shechinah* symbolizes God's nearness and is also referred to as *Malchut*, divine sovereignty.

Shefa: The divine radiant energy of *Ayn Sof* which flows along the twenty-two paths to the *sefirot*. The *sefirot*, in turn, mediate the blessings of the *Shefa* to our world below.

Shevirat Hakelim: "The Breaking of the Vessels." During Creation, the seven lower *sefirot* shattered because they could not contain the full radiant energy of the *Shefa*. This shattering caused the *netsotsot* to scatter and helps account for the initial misalignment of the *Etz Chayim*.

Shoresh neshamah: The root of our individual souls.

Siddur: Prayer book.

Sitra Achra: "The Other Side." The reality of evil pictured as the shadow, the mirror image of the *Etz Chayim*.

Three Levels of Soul: Derived from the three Hebrew words used for "spirit." *Nefesh* represents our creature vitality and instinct; *Ruach* is our emotional and social self; and *Neshamah* embodies our speculative reason, reflective self-consciousness, and high intuition.

Tiferet: Beauty. The beauty that emerges when *Chesed* and *Din* are in balance. In our unredeemed world, *Tiferet* embodies a yearning for completion and equilibrium.

Tikkun: The performance of God's commandments with the intent to elevate the *netsotsot* and help repair the cosmic fissures that occurred during *Shevirat Hakelim*.

Tselem: Envisioned by Kabbalists as an ethereal body, it is likened to a garment of our characteristics and experiences, which we weave through our deeds. Similar to the

Acquired Personality, it contains both the light of our higher traits and the *tsel*, the shadow side of our ignoble traits.

Yesod: Foundation. Also known as *Tsadik*, Righteous, because "the righteous are the foundation of the world" (Proverbs 10:25). *Yesod* focuses the divine energy, *Shefa*, from the higher *sefirot* and channels it downward. Also symbolizes the male generative organ when the *sefirot* are depicted in human form.

Yetser: "Inclination." According to rabbinic psychology, each individual has two inclinations. The *Yetser Ha Tov* is our Good Inclination, our altruistic drive. The *Yetser Ha Ra* is our Harmful Inclination, our drive toward self-aggrandizement at the expense of other people.

SUGGESTIONS FOR FURTHER READING

ENNEAGRAM

Adahan, Miriam. *Awareness.* New York: Feldheim, 1994.

Baron, R., and E. Wagele. *The Enneagram Made Easy.* San Francisco: HarperSanFrancisco, 1994.

The Enneagram Monthly. For information, call 877-428-9639.

Goldberg, Michael. *The Nine Ways of Working.* New York: Marlowe, 1999.

Mitrai, Sandra. *The Spiritual Dimensions of the Enneagram.* New York: Putnam, 2001.

Palmer, Helen. *The Enneagram.* San Francisco: HarperSanFrancisco, 1991.

———. *The Enneagram Advantage.* New York: Harmony, 1998.

———. *The Enneagram in Love and Work.* San Francisco: HarperSanFrancisco, 1995.

———. *The Pocket Enneagram.* San Francisco: HarperSanFrancisco, 1995.

Riso, Don Richard, with Russ Hudson. *Personality Types.* Revised edition. Boston: Houghton Mifflin, 1996.

Riso, Don Richard, with Russ Hudson. *The Wisdom of the Enneagram.* Boston: Houghton Mifflin, 2000.

Rohr, Richard, with Andreas Ebert. *Discovering the Enneagram.* New York: Crossroads, 1992.

Rohr, Richard. *Enneagram II.* New York: Crossroads, 1995.

Wagner, Jerome. *The Enneagram Spectrum of Personality Styles.* Portland, Ore.: Metamorphous Press, 1996.

Enneagram Personality Type Inventories

Aspell, P. J., and D. Aspell. *The Enneagram Inventory*. San Antonio, Texas: Life Wings, 1991.

Daniels, David, and Virginia Price. *The Essential Enneagram*. New York: HarperCollins, 2000.

Riso, Don Richard. *Discovering Your Personality Type*. Boston: Houghton Mifflin, 1995.

Wagner, Jerome. *Wagner Enneagram Personality Style Scales*. Western States Psychological Services, 1999.

On Line

Enneagram Institute (Riso/Hudson) www.enneagraminstitute.com

KABBALAH

Addison, Howard A. *The Enneagram and Kabbalah: Reading Your Soul*. Woodstock, Vt.: Jewish Lights, 1998.

Ariel, David. *The Mystic Quest*. Northvale, N. J.: Jason Aronson, 1988.

Buxbaum, Yitzhak. *Jewish Spiritual Practices*. Northvale, N. J.: Jason Aronson, 1990.

Cooper, David A. *The Handbook of Jewish Meditation Practices*. Woodstock, Vt.: Jewish Lights, 2000. Reprinted and updated from *Renewing Your Soul*. San Francisco: Harper-SanFrancisco, 1995.

———. *God Is a Verb*. New York: Riverhead, 1997.

Davis, Avram, ed. *Meditation from the Heart of Judaism: Today's Teachers Share Their Practices, Techniques, and Faith*. Woodstock, Vt.: Jewish Lights, 1997.

Dan, Joseph. *The Ancient Jewish Mysticism*. Tel Aviv: MOD Books, 1993.

Idel, Moshe. *Kabbalah: New Perspectives*. New Haven, Conn.: Yale University Press, 1988.

Kaplan, Aryeh. *Jewish Meditation*. New York: Schocken, 1985.

Kushner, Lawrence. *The Invisible Chariot*. Denver, Colo.: Alternatives in Religious Education, 1986.

———. *The Way Into Jewish Mystical Tradition*. Woodstock, Vt.: Jewish Lights, 2001.

Matt, Daniel C. *The Essential Kabbalah*. San Francisco: HarperSanFrancisco, 1996.

Scholem, Gershom. *Kabbalah*. New York: Times Books, 1974.

———. *Major Trends in Jewish Mysticism*. New York: Schocken, 1961.

About JEWISH LIGHTS Publishing

People of all faiths and backgrounds yearn for books that attract, engage, educate and spiritually inspire.

Our principal goal is to stimulate thought and help all people learn about who the Jewish People are, where they come from, and what the future can be made to hold. While people of our diverse Jewish heritage are the primary audience, our books speak to people in the Christian world as well and will broaden their understanding of Judaism and the roots of their own faith.

We bring to you authors who are at the forefront of spiritual thought and experience. While each has something different to say, they all say it in a voice that you can hear.

Our books are designed to welcome you and then to engage, stimulate and inspire. We judge our success not only by whether or not our books are beautiful and commercially successful, but by whether or not they make a difference in your life.

We at Jewish Lights take great care to produce beautiful books that present meaningful spiritual content in a form that reflects the art of making high quality books. Therefore, we want to acknowledge those who contributed to the production of this book.

Stuart M. Matlins, Publisher

PRODUCTION
Tim Holtz & Bridgett Taylor

EDITORIAL
Amanda Dupuis, Martha McKinney,
Polly Short Mahoney & Emily Wichland

COVER DESIGN
Lynne Walker, Lynne Walker Design Studio, Hanover, New Hampshire

TEXT DESIGN
Lisa Buckley, Lisa Buckley Design, San Francisco, California

COVER / TEXT PRINTING & BINDING
Lake Book, Melrose Park, Illinois

The Way Into... Series

A major 14-volume series to be completed over the next several years, **The Way Into...** provides an accessible and usable "guided tour" of the Jewish faith, its people, its history and beliefs—in total, an introduction to Judaism for adults that will enable them to understand and interact with sacred texts. Each volume is written by a major modern scholar and teacher, and is organized around an important concept of Judaism.

The Way Into... will enable all readers to achieve a real sense of Jewish cultural literacy through guided study. Available volumes include:

The Way Into Torah

by *Dr. Norman J. Cohen*

What is "Torah"? What are the different approaches to studying Torah? What are the different levels of understanding Torah? For whom is the study intended? Explores the origins and development of Torah, why it should be studied and how to do it.
6 x 9, 176 pp, HC, ISBN 1-58023-028-8 **$21.95**

The Way Into Jewish Prayer

by *Dr. Lawrence A. Hoffman*

Opens the door to 3,000 years of the Jewish way to God by making available all you need to feel at home in Jewish worship. Provides basic definitions of the terms you need to know as well as thoughtful analysis of the depth that lies beneath Jewish prayer.
6 x 9, 224 pp, HC, ISBN 1-58023-027-X **$21.95**

The Way Into Encountering God in Judaism

by *Dr. Neil Gillman*

Explains how Jews have encountered God throughout history—and today—by exploring the many metaphors for God in Jewish tradition. Explores the Jewish tradition's passionate but also conflicting ways of relating to God as Creator, relational partner, and a force in history and nature.
6 x 9, 240 pp, HC, ISBN 1-58023-025-3 **$21.95**

The Way Into Jewish Mystical Tradition

by *Rabbi Lawrence Kushner*

Explains the principles of Jewish mystical thinking, their religious and spiritual significance, and how they relate to our lives. A book that allows us to experience and understand the Jewish mystical approach to our place in the world.
6 x 9, 224 pp, HC, ISBN 1-58023-029-6 **$21.95**

Or phone, fax, mail or e-mail to: **JEWISH LIGHTS** Publishing
Sunset Farm Offices, Route 4 • P.O. Box 237 • Woodstock, Vermont 05091
Tel: (802) 457-4000 • Fax: (802) 457-4004 • www.jewishlights.com
Credit card orders: (800) 962-4544 (9AM–5PM ET Monday–Friday)
Generous discounts on quantity orders. SATISFACTION GUARANTEED. Prices subject to change.

Theology/Philosophy

Love and Terror in the God Encounter: *The Theological Legacy of Rabbi Joseph B. Soloveitchik, Vol. 1* by *Dr. David Hartman*

Renowned scholar David Hartman explores the sometimes surprising intersection of Soloveitchik's rootedness in halakhic tradition with his genuine responsiveness to modern Western theology. An engaging look at one of the most important Jewish thinkers of the twentieth century. 6 x 9, 240 pp, HC, ISBN 1-58023-112-8 **$25.00**

These Are the Words: *A Vocabulary of Jewish Spiritual Life*

by *Arthur Green*

What are the most essential ideas, concepts and terms that an educated person needs to know about Judaism? From *Adonai* (My Lord) to *zekhut* (merit), this enlightening and entertaining journey through Judaism teaches us the 149 core Hebrew words that constitute the basic vocabulary of Jewish spiritual life. 6 x 9, 304 pp, Quality PB, ISBN 1-58023-107-1 **$18.95**

Broken Tablets: *Restoring the Ten Commandments and Ourselves*

Ed. by *Rabbi Rachel S. Mikva*; Intro. by *Rabbi Lawrence Kushner* AWARD WINNER!

Twelve outstanding spiritual leaders each share profound and personal thoughts about these biblical commands and why they have such a special hold on us.
6 x 9, 192 pp, HC, ISBN 1-58023-066-0 **$21.95**

A Heart of Many Rooms: *Celebrating the Many Voices within Judaism* AWARD WINNER!
by Dr. David Hartman 6 x 9, 352 pp, HC, ISBN 1-58023-048-2 **$24.95**

A Living Covenant: *The Innovative Spirit in Traditional Judaism* AWARD WINNER!
by Dr. David Hartman 6 x 9, 368 pp, Quality PB, ISBN 1-58023-011-3 **$18.95**

Evolving Halakhah: *A Progressive Approach to Traditional Jewish Law*
by Rabbi Dr. Moshe Zemer 6 x 9, 480 pp, HC, ISBN 1-58023-002-4 **$40.00**

The Death of Death: *Resurrection and Immortality in Jewish Thought* AWARD WINNER!
by Dr. Neil Gillman 6 x 9, 336 pp, Quality PB, ISBN 1-58023-081-4 **$18.95**

The Last Trial: *On the Legends and Lore of the Command to Abraham to Offer Isaac as a Sacrifice* by Shalom Spiegel 6 x 9, 208 pp, Quality PB, ISBN 1-879045-29-X **$17.95**

Tormented Master: *The Life and Spiritual Quest of Rabbi Nahman of Bratslav*
by Dr. Arthur Green 6 x 9, 416 pp, Quality PB, ISBN 1-879045-11-7 **$18.95**

The Earth Is the Lord's: *The Inner World of the Jew in Eastern Europe*
by Abraham Joshua Heschel 5½ x 8, 128 pp, Quality PB, ISBN 1-879045-42-7 **$14.95**

A Passion for Truth: *Despair and Hope in Hasidism* by Abraham Joshua Heschel
5½ x 8, 352 pp, Quality PB, ISBN 1-879045-41-9 **$18.95**

Your Word Is Fire: *The Hasidic Masters on Contemplative Prayer* Ed. by Dr. Arthur Green and Dr. Barry W. Holtz 6 x 9, 160 pp, Quality PB, ISBN 1-879045-25-7 **$14.95**

Spirituality

My People's Prayer Book: *Traditional Prayers, Modern Commentaries*
Ed. by *Dr. Lawrence A. Hoffman*

Provides a diverse and exciting commentary to the traditional liturgy, helping modern men and women find new wisdom in Jewish prayer, and bring liturgy into their lives. Each book includes Hebrew text, modern translation, and commentaries *from all perspectives* of the Jewish world.

Vol. 1—*The Sh'ma and Its Blessings*, 7 x 10, 168 pp, HC, ISBN 1-879045-79-6 **$23.95**
Vol. 2—*The Amidah*, 7 x 10, 240 pp, HC, ISBN 1-879045-80-X **$23.95**
Vol. 3—*P'sukei D'zimrah* (Morning Psalms), 7 x 10, 240 pp, HC, ISBN 1-879045-81-8 **$24.95**
Vol. 4—*Seder K'riat Hatorah* (The Torah Service), 7 x 10, 264 pp, ISBN 1-879045-82-6 **$23.95**
Vol. 5—*Birkhot Hashachar* (Morning Blessings), 7 x 10, 256 pp, ISBN 1-879045-83-4 **$24.95**

Becoming a Congregation of Learners
Learning as a Key to Revitalizing Congregational Life by Isa Aron, Ph.D.;
Foreword by Rabbi Lawrence A. Hoffman, Co-Developer, Synagogue 2000
6 x 9, 304 pp, Quality PB, ISBN 1-58023-089-X **$19.95**

Self, Struggle & Change
Family Conflict Stories in Genesis and Their Healing Insights for Our Lives
by Dr. Norman J. Cohen 6 x 9, 224 pp, Quality PB, ISBN 1-879045-66-4 **$16.95**;
HC, ISBN 1-879045-19-2 **$21.95**

Voices from Genesis: *Guiding Us through the Stages of Life*
by Dr. Norman J. Cohen 6 x 9, 192 pp, Quality PB, ISBN 1-58023-118-7 **$16.95**;
HC, ISBN 1-879045-75-3 **$21.95**

God Whispers: *Stories of the Soul, Lessons of the Heart*
by Rabbi Karyn D. Kedar 6 x 9, 176 pp, Quality PB, ISBN 1-58023-088-1 **$15.95**

The Business Bible: *10 New Commandments for Bringing Spirituality & Ethical Values into the Workplace*
by Rabbi Wayne Dosick 5½ x 8½, 208 pp, Quality PB, ISBN 1-58023-101-2 **$14.95**

Being God's Partner: *How to Find the Hidden Link Between Spirituality and Your Work*
by Rabbi Jeffrey K. Salkin; Intro. by Norman Lear **AWARD WINNER!**
6 x 9, 192 pp, Quality PB, ISBN 1-879045-65-6 **$16.95**; HC, ISBN 1-879045-37-0 **$19.95**

God & the Big Bang
Discovering Harmony Between Science & Spirituality **AWARD WINNER!**
by Daniel C. Matt 6 x 9, 224 pp, Quality PB, ISBN 1-879045-89-3 **$16.95**

Soul Judaism: *Dancing with God into a New Era*
by Rabbi Wayne Dosick 5½ x 8½, 304 pp, Quality PB, ISBN 1-58023-053-9 **$16.95**

Finding Joy: *A Practical Spiritual Guide to Happiness* **AWARD WINNER!**
by Rabbi Dannel I. Schwartz with Mark Hass
6 x 9, 192 pp, Quality PB, ISBN 1-58023-009-1 **$14.95**; HC, ISBN 1-879045-53-2 **$19.95**

Healing/Wellness/Recovery

Jewish Paths toward Healing and Wholeness
A Personal Guide to Dealing with Suffering
by *Rabbi Kerry M. Olitzky*; Foreword by *Debbie Friedman*

Why me? Why do we suffer? How can we heal? Grounded in personal experience with illness and Jewish spiritual traditions, this book provides healing rituals, psalms and prayers that help readers initiate a dialogue with God, to guide them along the complicated path of healing and wholeness. 6 x 9, 192 pp, Quality PB, ISBN 1-58023-068-7 **$15.95**

Healing of Soul, Healing of Body
Spiritual Leaders Unfold the Strength & Solace in Psalms
Ed. by *Rabbi Simkha Y. Weintraub*, CSW, for The National Center for Jewish Healing

A source of solace for those who are facing illness, as well as those who care for them. Provides a wellspring of strength with inspiring introductions and commentaries by eminent spiritual leaders reflecting all Jewish movements.
6 x 9, 128 pp, Quality PB, Illus., 2-color text, ISBN 1-879045-31-1 **$14.95**

Jewish Pastoral Care
A Practical Handbook from Traditional and Contemporary Sources
Ed. by *Rabbi Dayle A. Friedman*

Gives today's Jewish pastoral counselors practical guidelines based in the Jewish tradition.
6 x 9, 464 pp, HC, ISBN 1-58023-078-4 **$35.00**

Twelve Jewish Steps to Recovery: *A Personal Guide to Turning from Alcoholism & Other Addictions . . . Drugs, Food, Gambling, Sex . . .* by Rabbi Kerry M. Olitzky & Stuart A. Copans, M.D. Preface by Abraham J. Twerski, M.D.; Intro. by Rabbi Sheldon Zimmerman; "Getting Help" by JACS Foundation 6 x 9, 144 pp, Quality PB, ISBN 1-879045-09-5 **$13.95**

One Hundred Blessings Every Day: *Daily Twelve Step Recovery Affirmations, Exercises for Personal Growth & Renewal Reflecting Seasons of the Jewish Year*
by Rabbi Kerry M. Olitzky 4½ x 6½, 432 pp, Quality PB, ISBN 1-879045-30-3 **$14.95**

Recovery from Codependence: *A Jewish Twelve Steps Guide to Healing Your Soul*
by Rabbi Kerry M. Olitzky 6 x 9, 160 pp, Quality PB, ISBN 1-879045-32-X **$13.95**;
HC, ISBN 1-879045-27-3 **$21.95**

Renewed Each Day: *Daily Twelve Step Recovery Meditations Based on the Bible*
by Rabbi Kerry M. Olitzky & Aaron Z. *Vol. I: Genesis & Exodus*; *Vol. II: Leviticus, Numbers and Deuteronomy*
Vol. I: 6 x 9, 224 pp, Quality PB, ISBN 1-879045-12-5 **$14.95**
Vol. II: 6 x 9, 280 pp, Quality PB, ISBN 1-879045-13-3 **$14.95**

Children's Spirituality

In Our Image
God's First Creatures
by *Nancy Sohn Swartz*

Full-color illus. by *Melanie Hall*

For ages 4 & up

A playful new twist on the Creation story—from the perspective of the animals. Celebrates the interconnectedness of nature and the harmony of all living things. "The vibrantly colored illustrations nearly leap off the page in this delightful interpretation." —*School Library Journal*

9 x 12, 32 pp, HC, Full-color illus., ISBN 1-879045-99-0 **$16.95**

God's Paintbrush
by *Sandy Eisenberg Sasso*; Full-color illus. by *Annette Compton*

For ages 4 & up

Invites children of all faiths and backgrounds to encounter God openly in their own lives. Wonderfully interactive; provides questions adult and child can explore together at the end of each episode.
11 x 8½, 32 pp, HC, Full-color illus., ISBN 1-879045-22-2 **$16.95**

Also available: A Teacher's Guide: A Guide for Jewish & Christian Educators and Parents
8½ x 11, 32 pp, PB, ISBN 1-879045-57-5 **$8.95**

God's Paintbrush Celebration Kit 9½ x 12, HC, Includes 5 sessions/40 full-color Activity Sheets and Teacher Folder with complete instructions, ISBN 1-58023-050-4 **$21.95**

In God's Name
by *Sandy Eisenberg Sasso*; Full-color illus. by *Phoebe Stone*

For ages 4 & up

Like an ancient myth in its poetic text and vibrant illustrations, this award-winning modern fable about the search for God's name celebrates the diversity and, at the same time, the unity of all the people of the world.
9 x 12, 32 pp, HC, Full-color illus., ISBN 1-879045-26-5 **$16.95**

What Is God's Name? (A Board Book)

For ages 0–4

An abridged board book version of the award-winning *In God's Name*.
5 x 5, 24 pp, Board, Full-color illus., ISBN 1-893361-10-1 **$7.95** A SKYLIGHT PATHS Book

The 11th Commandment: Wisdom from Our Children
by *The Children of America*

For all ages

"If there were an Eleventh Commandment, what would it be?" Children of many religious denominations across America answer this question—in their own drawings and words. "A rare book of spiritual celebration for all people, of all ages, for all time."—*Bookviews*
8 x 10, 48 pp, HC, Full-color illus., ISBN 1-879045-46-X **$16.95**

Children's Spirituality

God Said Amen
by *Sandy Eisenberg Sasso*
Full-color illus. by *Avi Katz*

For ages
4 & up

A warm and inspiring tale of two kingdoms: one overflowing with water but without oil to light its lamps; the other blessed with oil but no water to grow its gardens. The kingdoms' rulers ask God for help but are too stubborn to ask each other. It takes a minstrel, a pair of royal riding-birds and their young keepers, and a simple act of kindness to show that they need only reach out to each other to find God's answer to their prayers.

9 x 12, 32 pp, HC, Full-color illus., ISBN 1-58023-080-6 **$16.95**

For Heaven's Sake
by *Sandy Eisenberg Sasso*; Full-color illus. by *Kathryn Kunz Finney*

For ages
4 & up

Everyone talked about heaven: "Thank heavens." "Heaven forbid." "For heaven's sake, Isaiah." But no one would say what heaven was or how to find it. So Isaiah decides to find out, by seeking answers from many different people.
9 x 12, 32 pp, HC, Full-color illus., ISBN 1-58023-054-7 **$16.95**

But God Remembered
Stories of Women from Creation to the Promised Land

For ages
8 & up

by *Sandy Eisenberg Sasso*; Full-color illus. by *Bethanne Andersen*

A fascinating collection of four different stories of women only briefly mentioned in biblical tradition and religious texts. Vibrantly brings to life courageous and strong women from ancient tradition; all teach important values through their actions and faith.
9 x 12, 32 pp, HC, Full-color illus., ISBN 1-879045-43-5 **$16.95**

God in Between
by *Sandy Eisenberg Sasso*; Full-color illus. by *Sally Sweetland*

For ages
4 & up

If you wanted to find God, where would you look? A magical, mythical tale that teaches that God can be found where we are: within all of us and the relationships between us.
9 x 12, 32 pp, HC, Full-color illus., ISBN 1-879045-86-9 **$16.95**

For ages
4 & up

A Prayer for the Earth: The Story of Naamah, Noah's Wife
by *Sandy Eisenberg Sasso*; Full-color illus. by *Bethanne Andersen*

This new story, based on an ancient text, opens readers' religious imaginations to new ideas about the well-known story of the Flood. When God tells Noah to bring the animals of the world onto the ark, God also calls on Naamah, Noah's wife, to save each plant on Earth.
9 x 12, 32 pp, HC, Full-color illus., ISBN 1-879045-60-5 **$16.95**

Children's Spirituality

Because Nothing Looks Like God
by *Lawrence and Karen Kushner*
Full-color illus. by *Dawn W. Majewski*

For ages 4 & up

MULTICULTURAL, NONDENOMINATIONAL, NONSECTARIAN

What is God like? The first collaborative work by husband-and-wife team Lawrence and Karen Kushner introduces children to the possibilities of spiritual life. Real-life examples of happiness and sadness—from goodnight stories, to the hope and fear felt the first time at bat, to the closing moments of life—invite us to explore, together with our children, the questions we all have about God, no matter what our age.

11 x 8½, 32 pp, HC, Full-color illus., ISBN 1-58023-092-X **$16.95**

Where Is God?
What Does God Look Like?
How Does God Make Things Happen? (Board Books)

For ages 0–4

by *Lawrence and Karen Kushner*; Full-color illus. by *Dawn W. Majewski*

Gently invites children to become aware of God's presence all around them. Three board books abridged from *Because Nothing Looks Like God* by Lawrence and Karen Kushner.
Each 5 x 5, 24 pp, Board, Full-color illus. **$7.95**   SKYLIGHT PATHS Books

Sharing Blessings
Children's Stories for Exploring the Spirit of the Jewish Holidays
by *Rahel Musleah* and *Rabbi Michael Klayman*
Full-color illus. by *Mary O'Keefe Young*

For ages 6 & up

What is the spiritual message of each of the Jewish holidays? How do we teach it to our children? Many books tell children about the historical significance and customs of the holidays. Through stories about one family's preparation, *Sharing Blessings* explores ways to get into the *spirit* of 13 different holidays.
8½ x 11, 64 pp, HC, Full-color illus., ISBN 1-879045-71-0 **$18.95**

The Book of Miracles
A Young Person's Guide to Jewish Spiritual Awareness
by *Lawrence Kushner*

For ages 9 & up

Introduces kids to a way of everyday spiritual thinking to last a lifetime. Kushner, whose award-winning books have brought spirituality to life for countless adults, now shows young people how to use Judaism as a foundation on which to build their lives.
6 x 9, 96 pp, HC, 2-color illus., ISBN 1-879045-78-8 **$16.95**

Spirituality—The Kushner Series
Books by Lawrence Kushner

The Way Into Jewish Mystical Tradition

Explains the principles of Jewish mystical thinking, their religious and spiritual significance, and how they relate to our lives. A book that allows us to experience and understand the Jewish mystical approach to our place in the world. 6 x 9, 224 pp, HC, ISBN 1-58023-029-6 **$21.95**

Eyes Remade for Wonder
The Way of Jewish Mysticism and Sacred Living

A Lawrence Kushner Reader Intro. by *Thomas Moore*

Whether you are new to Kushner or a devoted fan, you'll find inspiration here. With samplings from each of Kushner's works, and a generous amount of new material, this book is to be read and reread, each time discovering deeper layers of meaning in our lives.
6 x 9, 240 pp, Quality PB, ISBN 1-58023-042-3 **$16.95**; HC, ISBN 1-58023-014-8 **$23.95**

Because Nothing Looks Like God

by *Lawrence and Karen Kushner*; Full-color illus. by *Dawn W. Majewski*

What is God like? The first collaborative work by husband-and-wife team Lawrence and Karen Kushner introduces children to the possibilities of spiritual life with three poetic spiritual stories. Real-life examples of happiness and sadness—from goodnight stories, to the hope and fear felt the first time at bat, to the closing moments of life—invite us to explore, together with our children, the questions we all have about God, no matter what our age. **For ages 4 & up**
11 x 8½, 32 pp, HC, Full-color illus., ISBN 1-58023-092-X **$16.95**

Invisible Lines of Connection: *Sacred Stories of the Ordinary* AWARD WINNER!
6 x 9, 160 pp, Quality PB, ISBN 1-879045-98-2 **$15.95**; HC, ISBN 1-879045-52-4 **$21.95**

Honey from the Rock: *An Introduction to Jewish Mysticism* SPECIAL ANNIVERSARY EDITION
6 x 9, 176 pp, Quality PB, ISBN 1-58023-073-3 **$15.95**

The Book of Letters: *A Mystical Hebrew Alphabet* AWARD WINNER!
Popular HC Edition, 6 x 9, 80 pp, 2-color text, ISBN 1-879045-00-1 **$24.95**; *Deluxe Gift Edition,* 9 x 12, 80 pp, HC, 2-color text, ornamentation, slipcase, ISBN 1-879045-01-X **$79.95**; *Collector's Limited Edition,* 9 x 12, 80 pp, HC, gold-embossed pages, hand-assembled slipcase. With silkscreened print. Limited to 500 signed and numbered copies, ISBN 1-879045-04-4 **$349.00**

The Book of Words: *Talking Spiritual Life, Living Spiritual Talk* AWARD WINNER!
6 x 9, 160 pp, Quality PB, 2-color text, ISBN 1-58023-020-2 **$16.95**;
152 pp, HC, ISBN 1-879045-35-4 **$21.95**

God Was in This Place & I, i Did Not Know
Finding Self, Spirituality and Ultimate Meaning
6 x 9, 192 pp, Quality PB, ISBN 1-879045-33-8 **$16.95**

The River of Light: *Jewish Mystical Awareness* SPECIAL ANNIVERSARY EDITION
6 x 9, 192 pp, Quality PB, ISBN 1-58023-096-2 **$16.95**

Women's Spirituality / Ecology

Torah of the Earth: *Exploring 4,000 Years of Ecology in Jewish Thought*
In 2 Volumes Ed. by *Rabbi Arthur Waskow*

Major new resource offering us an invaluable key to understanding the intersection of ecology and Judaism. Leading scholars provide us with a guided tour of ecological thought from four major Jewish viewpoints.
Vol. 1: *Biblical Israel & Rabbinic Judaism,* 6 x 9, 272 pp, Quality PB, ISBN 1-58023-086-5 **$19.95**
Vol. 2: *Zionism & Eco-Judaism,* 6 x 9, 336 pp, Quality PB, ISBN 1-58023-087-3 **$19.95**

Ecology & the Jewish Spirit: *Where Nature & the Sacred Meet* Ed. and with Intros.
by Ellen Bernstein 6 x 9, 288 pp, Quality PB, ISBN 1-58023-082-2 **$16.95**;
HC, ISBN 1-879045-88-5 **$23.95**

The Jewish Gardening Cookbook: *Growing Plants & Cooking for Holidays & Festivals*
by Michael Brown 6 x 9, 224 pp, Illus., Quality PB, ISBN 1-58023-116-0 **$16.95**;
HC, ISBN 1-58023-004-0 **$21.95**

Moonbeams: *A Hadassah Rosh Hodesh Guide*

Ed. by *Carol Diament, Ph.D.*

This hands-on "idea book" focuses on *Rosh Hodesh*, the festival of the new moon, as a source of spiritual growth for Jewish women. A complete sourcebook that will initiate or rejuvenate women's study groups, it is also perfect for women preparing for *bat mitzvah*, or for anyone interested in learning more about *Rosh Hodesh* observance and what it has to offer. 8½ x 11, 240 pp, Quality PB, ISBN 1-58023-099-7 **$20.00**

The Women's Torah Commentary: *New Insights from Women Rabbis on the 54 Weekly Torah Portions* Ed. by *Rabbi Elyse Goldstein*

For the first time, women rabbis provide a commentary on the entire Five Books of Moses. More than 25 years after the first woman was ordained a rabbi in America, these inspiring teachers bring their rich perspectives to bear on the biblical text. In a week-by-week format; a perfect gift for others, or for yourself. 6 x 9, 496 pp, HC, ISBN 1-58023-076-8 **$34.95**

Lifecycles, in Two Volumes AWARD WINNERS!
V. 1: *Jewish Women on Life Passages & Personal Milestones*
Ed. and with Intros. by Rabbi Debra Orenstein
V. 2: *Jewish Women on Biblical Themes in Contemporary Life*
Ed. and with Intros. by Rabbi Debra Orenstein and Rabbi Jane Rachel Litman
V. 1: 6 x 9, 480 pp, Quality PB, ISBN 1-58023-018-0 **$19.95**; HC, ISBN 1-879045-14-1 **$24.95**
V. 2: 6 x 9, 464 pp, Quality PB, ISBN 1-58023-019-9 **$19.95**

ReVisions: *Seeing Torah through a Feminist Lens* AWARD WINNER!
by Rabbi Elyse Goldstein 5½ x 8½, 224 pp, Quality PB, ISBN 1-58023-117-9 **$16.95**;
208 pp, HC, ISBN 1-58023-047-4 **$19.95**

The Year Mom Got Religion: *One Woman's Midlife Journey into Judaism*
by Lee Meyerhoff Hendler 6 x 9, 208 pp, Quality PB, ISBN 1-58023-070-9 **$15.95**

Spirituality/Jewish Meditation

Discovering Jewish Meditation
Instruction & Guidance for Learning an Ancient Spiritual Practice
by *Nan Fink Gefen*

Gives readers of any level of understanding the tools to learn the practice of Jewish meditation on your own, starting you on the path to a deep spiritual and personal connection to God and to greater insight about your life. 6 x 9, 208 pp, Quality PB, ISBN 1-58023-067-9 **$16.95**

Entering the Temple of Dreams: *Jewish Prayers, Movements, and Meditations for the End of the Day* by *Tamar Frankiel* and *Judy Greenfeld*

Nighttime spirituality is much more than bedtime prayers! Here, you'll uncover deeper meaning to familiar nighttime prayers—and learn to combine the prayers with movements and meditations to enhance your physical and psychological well-being.
7 x 10, 192 pp, Quality PB, Illus., ISBN 1-58023-079-2 **$16.95**

One God Clapping: *The Spiritual Path of a Zen Rabbi* Award Winner!
by *Alan Lew* with *Sherril Jaffe*

A fascinating personal story of a Jewish meditation expert's roundabout spiritual journey from Zen Buddhist practitioner to rabbi. 5½ x 8½, 336 pp, Quality PB, ISBN 1-58023-115-2 **$16.95**

 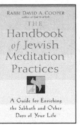 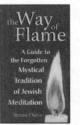  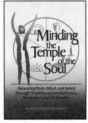

The Handbook of Jewish Meditation Practices
A Guide for Enriching the Sabbath and Other Days of Your Life
by *Rabbi David A. Cooper*

Gives us ancient and modern Jewish tools—Jewish practices and traditions, easy-to-use meditation exercises, and contemplative study of Jewish sacred texts. 6 x 9, 208 pp, Quality PB, ISBN 1-58023-102-0 **$16.95**

Stepping Stones to Jewish Spiritual Living: *Walking the Path Morning, Noon, and Night*
by Rabbi James L. Mirel & Karen Bonnell Werth
6 x 9, 240 pp, Quality PB, ISBN 1-58023-074-1 **$16.95**

Meditation from the Heart of Judaism
Today's Teachers Share Their Practices, Techniques, and Faith
Ed. by Avram Davis 6 x 9, 256 pp, Quality PB, ISBN 1-58023-049-0 **$16.95**;
HC, ISBN 1-879045-77-X **$21.95**

The Way of Flame: *A Guide to the Forgotten Mystical Tradition of Jewish Meditation*
by Avram Davis 4½ x 8, 176 pp, Quality PB, ISBN 1-58023-060-1 **$15.95**

Minding the Temple of the Soul: *Balancing Body, Mind, and Spirit through Traditional Jewish Prayer, Movement, and Meditation*
by Tamar Frankiel and Judy Greenfeld 7 x 10, 184 pp, Quality PB, Illus.,
ISBN 1-879045-64-8 **$16.95**; Audiotape of the Blessings and Meditations (60-min. cassette), JN01 **$9.95**; Videotape of the Movements and Meditations (46-min.), S507 **$20.00**

Spirituality & More

The Jewish Lights Spirituality Handbook
A Guide to Understanding, Exploring & Living a Spiritual Life
Ed. by *Stuart M. Matlins, Editor-in-Chief, Jewish Lights Publishing*

Rich, creative material from over 50 spiritual leaders on every aspect of Jewish spirituality today: prayer, meditation, mysticism, study, rituals, special days, the everyday, and more.
6 x 9, 456 pp, Quality PB, ISBN 1-58023-093-8 **$18.95**; HC, ISBN 1-58023-100-4 **$24.95**

Six Jewish Spiritual Paths: *A Rationalist Looks at Spirituality*
by *Rabbi Rifat Sonsino*

The quest for spirituality is universal, but which path to spirituality is right *for you?* A straight-forward, objective discussion of the many ways—each valid and authentic—for seekers to gain a richer spiritual life within Judaism. 6 x 9, 208 pp, HC, ISBN 1-58023-095-4 **$21.95**

Criminal Kabbalah
An Intriguing Anthology of Jewish Mystery & Detective Fiction
Edited by *Lawrence W. Raphael*; Foreword by *Laurie R. King*

Twelve of today's best known mystery authors provide an intriguing collection of new stories sure to enlighten at the same time they entertain.
6 x 9, 256 pp, Quality PB, ISBN 1-58023-109-8 **$16.95**

Mystery Midrash: *An Anthology of Jewish Mystery & Detective Fiction* AWARD WINNER!
Ed. by Lawrence W. Raphael 6 x 9, 304 pp, Quality PB, ISBN 1-58023-055-5 **$16.95**

Sacred Intentions: *Daily Inspiration to Strengthen the Spirit, Based on Jewish Wisdom*
by Rabbi Kerry M. Olitzky & Rabbi Lori Forman
4½ x 6½, 448 pp, Quality PB, ISBN 1-58023-061-X **$15.95**

Restful Reflections: *Nighttime Inspiration to Calm the Soul, Based on Jewish Wisdom*
by Rabbi Kerry M. Olitzky & Rabbi Lori Forman
4½ x 6½, 448 pp, Quality PB, ISBN 1-58023-091-1 **$15.95**

The Enneagram and Kabbalah: *Reading Your Soul*
by Rabbi Howard A. Addison 6 x 9, 176 pp, Quality PB, ISBN 1-58023-001-6 **$15.95**

Embracing the Covenant: *Converts to Judaism Talk About Why & How*
Ed. and with Intros. by Rabbi Allan L. Berkowitz and Patti Moskovitz
6 x 9, 192 pp, Quality PB, ISBN 1-879045-50-8 **$15.95**

Wandering Stars: *An Anthology of Jewish Fantasy & Science Fiction* Ed. by Jack Dann;
Intro. by Isaac Asimov 6 x 9, 272 pp, Quality PB, ISBN 1-58023-005-9 **$16.95**

Israel—A Spiritual Travel Guide AWARD WINNER!
A Companion for the Modern Jewish Pilgrim
by Rabbi Lawrence A. Hoffman 4¾ x 10, 256 pp, Quality PB, ISBN 1-879045-56-7 **$18.95**

AVAILABLE FROM BETTER BOOKSTORES. TRY YOUR BOOKSTORE FIRST.

Spirituality

Does the Soul Survive?
A Jewish Journey to Belief in Afterlife, Past Lives & Living with Purpose
by *Rabbi Elie Kaplan Spitz*; Foreword by *Brian L. Weiss, M.D.*

Spitz relates his own experiences and those shared with him by people he has worked with as a rabbi, and shows us that belief in afterlife and past lives, so often approached with reluctance, is in fact true to Jewish tradition. 6 x 9, 288 pp, HC, ISBN 1-58023-094-6 **$21.95**

The Women's Torah Commentary: *New Insights from Women Rabbis on the 54 Weekly Torah Portions* Ed. by *Rabbi Elyse Goldstein*

For the first time, women rabbis provide a commentary on the entire Torah. In a week-by-week format; a perfect gift for others, or for yourself.
6 x 9, 496 pp, HC, ISBN 1-58023-076-8 **$34.95**

The Gift of Kabbalah
Discovering the Secrets of Heaven, Renewing Your Life on Earth
by *Tamar Frankiel, Ph.D.*

Makes accessible the mysteries of Kabbalah. Traces Kabbalah's evolution in Judaism and shows us its most important gift: a way of revealing the connection between our "everyday" life and the spiritual oneness of the universe. 6 x 9, 256 pp, HC, ISBN 1-58023-108-X **$21.95**

Bringing the Psalms to Life: *How to Understand and Use the Book of Psalms*
by Rabbi Daniel F. Polish 6 x 9, 208 pp, Quality PB, ISBN 1-58023-157-8 **$16.95**;
HC, ISBN 1-58023-077-6 **$21.95**

The Empty Chair: *Finding Hope and Joy—*
Timeless Wisdom from a Hasidic Master, Rebbe Nachman of Breslov AWARD WINNER!
4 x 6, 128 pp, Deluxe PB, 2-color text, ISBN 1-879045-67-2 **$9.95**

The Gentle Weapon: *Prayers for Everyday and Not-So-Everyday Moments*
Adapted from the Wisdom of Rebbe Nachman of Breslov
4 x 6, 144 pp, Deluxe PB, 2-color text, ISBN 1-58023-022-9 **$9.95**

Ancient Secrets: *Using the Stories of the Bible to Improve Our Everyday Lives*
by Rabbi Levi Meier, Ph.D. 5½ x 8½, 288 pp, Quality PB, ISBN 1-58023-064-4 **$16.95**

Or phone, fax, mail or e-mail to: **JEWISH LIGHTS Publishing**
Sunset Farm Offices, Route 4 • P.O. Box 237 • Woodstock, Vermont 05091
Tel: (802) 457-4000 • Fax: (802) 457-4004 • www.jewishlights.com
Credit card orders: (800) 962-4544 (9AM–5PM ET Monday–Friday)
Generous discounts on quantity orders. SATISFACTION GUARANTEED. Prices subject to change.